ACPL, Laramie, WY   12/2016
39092055358289
Harik, Ramsay M.
Women in the Middle East : tradition and
Pieces: 1

D0122307

ALBANY COUNTY
PUBLIC LIBRARY
Serving the Laramie Plains since 1887

Laramie, Wyoming 82070

IN HONOR OF

The Acpl Staff

Women
in the Middle East

Women
in the Middle East
Tradition and Change
REVISED EDITION

Ramsay M. Harik and Elsa Marston

Franklin Watts
A Division of Scholastic Inc.
New York • Toronto • London • Auckland • Sydney
Mexico City • New Delhi • Hong Kong
Danbury, Connecticut

ALBANY COUNTY
PUBLIC LIBRARY
LARAMIE, WYOMING

Photographs © 2003: AP/Wide World Photos: 138 (Adam Butler), 79 (Victor R. Caivano), 135 (Charles Dharapak), 154, 157 (Kamran Jebreili), 140 (Hussein Malla), 85 (Hasan Sarbakhshian), 94 (Marud Sezer), 52 (Mohamed Zatari); Barbara Nimri Aziz: 10, 103; Corbis Images: 119 (Joseph Barrak/AFP), 75, 88 (Bettmann), 156 (Peter Turnley); Corbis Sygma: 117 (Vo Trung Dung), cover, spot art, 3 (John Van Hasselt), 37, 129; Elizabeth Wicket: 19; Elsa Marston: 30, 32, 66, 69, 78, 104, 112, 123, 165; Folio, Inc./Fred J. Maroon: 113; Getty Images/Abid Katib: 131; Impact Visuals/Donna DeCesare: 41, 96; Islamic Home for the Disabled: 147; Magnum Photos/Abbas: 51; Panos Pictures/Giacomo Pirozzi: 24, 34; Peter Arnold Inc.: 23 (Glen Christian/Lineair), 73 (Neil Cooper); Photo Researchers, NY: 28, 59 (George Chan), 58 (Richard T. Nowitz); Sipa Press/Petra/AAR: 127; Sovfoto/Eastfoto: 14 (Itar-Tass); Stock Boston/Sean Sprague: 8; Superstock, Inc.: 101; Thomas Hartwell: 15; TRIP Photo Library/H. Rogers: 11; Tunisian Association of Democratic Women: 63; United Nations/DPI: 21, 61; Woodfin Camp & Associates: 80 (Barry Iverson), 67.

Book design by A. Natacha Pimentel C.

Library of Congress Cataloging-in-Publication Data

Harik, Ramsay M.
    Women in the Middle East : tradition and change / Ramsay M. Harik and Elsa Marston. — Rev. ed.
        p. cm. — Includes bibliographical references and index.
        ISBN 0-531-12222-0
1. Women—Middle East—Social conditions—Juvenile literature. [1. Women—Middle East—Social conditions.] I. Marston, Elsa. II. Title.
        HQ1726.5 .H37 2003
        305.42′0956—dc21

Copyright © 2003 Ramsay M. Harik and Elsa Marston
All rights reserved. Printed in the United States of America.
Published simultaneously in Canada.
    2 3 4 5 6 7 8 9 10 R 12 11 10 09 08 07 06 05 04 03

Contents

Foreword

*I*n the first edition of this book, published in 1996, we hoped to encourage an accurate and up-to-date view of Middle Eastern women's lives, guiding the reader toward an acquaintance with people of the Middle East as *people*, not just social categories. While that is still our primary objective in this edition, we have also sought to trace developments in certain areas of social change and have added new chapters on health, women's movements, and the recent experience of women in Afghanistan. We have tried to include at least a few illustrations from every country in the region—always feeling that whatever we say about the lives of women in the Middle East and North Africa, we are merely scratching the surface of an infinitely complex and interesting reality.

This updated edition benefits almost equally from recent research by scholars and topical reports and articles. As earlier, our personal contacts and interviews in both the United States and in Lebanon, Egypt, and Tunisia have been invaluable in helping us understand better and in providing real-life illustrations. We deeply appreciate the help of many individuals and wish that space permitted us to mention them all by name.

Shopping on a breezy day in Morocco.

Women of the Middle East

Life is full of unhappiness, and most of it caused by women.
—Lebanese proverb

In this world only three things dispel anxiety: horses, books, and women.
—Arabic proverb

What images come to mind with the words *Middle Eastern women?* Exotic harems of mysterious beauties, or Bedouin women living in desert tents? Silent creatures, completely enveloped in black robes? For many Americans, these are typical images—picked up from fiction, movies, and the news media.

Yet, like all stereotypes, these images limit and distort our understanding. In today's Middle East, women play a great many roles and have much to say about their own lives and futures. Some are doctors, teachers, business entrepreneurs, artists, farmers, cab drivers, and even soldiers. Others remain in the more traditional realm as wives, mothers, and daughters; many carry on both career and domestic roles. Yet almost all are affected by tremendous social changes. In this book we will explore these roles to gain an appreciation of the opportunities and challenges women face in the Middle East today.

Tradition and Change

Much of the challenge comes from the fact that the Middle East, like many regions in the world, is caught in the tension between tradition and change. Middle Eastern people are proud of their rich cultural traditions, which give them strength and identity in an often hostile world. They also realize that they must adapt to the modern world if they are to survive economically and politically. In large part, what is happening today is the story of these people's struggle to find the right balance and define their identity.

Women are particularly affected by this tension. Some of the more conservative traditions of the Middle East have had the effect of keeping women severely oppressed. At the same time, some changes brought on by modernization may impose burdens on women's lives. The "proper" role of women in society has become a battleground between the guardians of the old ways and the proponents of the new, with women themselves too often denied a voice concerning their own destinies. Yet many are confronting this dilemma, creating new identities as women both modern and true to their culture.

Students between classes at a vocational school in Iraq

Defining the "Middle East"

The origins of the term "Middle East" are actually European. To Europeans in the past, everything between Turkey and Japan was the "East" or the "Orient." Japan and China were the "Far East," and the eastern Mediterranean world was the "Middle" or "Near East." The lands and societies of Europe and America became known as the "West."

Simply for ease in reading, this book uses the term Middle East to include the countries of North Africa. Thus we define the area as the cultural region stretching from Morocco in the west to Iran in the east. It includes 20 nations and perhaps 290 million people, about the same population as the United States. Its topography ranges from the rugged, snowy mountains of Morocco, Lebanon, and Iran, to the fertile Nile delta and the vast deserts of Saudi Arabia. It is a world of tiny fishing villages and sprawling cities, of Bedouin encampments and silver Rolls-Royces. Its people vary from the blue-eyed Berbers of North Africa to the black Nubians of Upper Egypt.

With such diversity, what justifies our calling this region by one unifying name, the Middle East? The key is in the term *cultural region.* Although the Middle East contains many ethnic groups, they share enough cultural forms for their similarities often to outweigh their differences.

Perhaps the most prominent cultural factor is religion. In the seventh century C.E., inspired by their dynamic new religion of Islam, the tribes of Arabia joined together and swept through what today we call the Middle East, bringing their religion,

Egyptian women washing clothes along the Nile

language, and culture to populations from Persia to North Africa. It is for this historic reason that today the Middle East is largely associated with Arabs and Islam.

The unifying power of Islamic belief and culture has been tremendous. Islam is not simply a personal religion but a way of life and a way of organizing society to support that way of life. It is fundamentally a public and *shared* religion, in which believers participate daily and thus find a common bond.

The Middle East and the West

Historically, encounters between the largely Muslim Middle East and neighboring Christian Europe resulted in misunderstanding and hostility. This history of confrontation has given Middle Easterners another common bond.

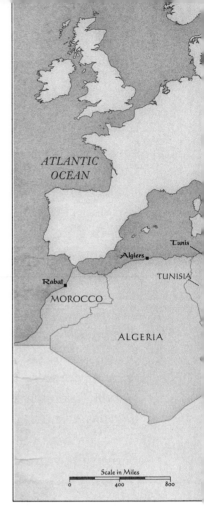

The last 200 years or so, Western ways of organizing government, economics, and society have come to define the modern world, with huge impact on other cultures. The West's attempts to impose its ways on the traditional Arab world have been a source of tension between the two great cultures since the time of the Crusades in the twelfth and thirteenth centuries.

The Middle East's glory days, when Europe was comparatively backward, lasted from the eighth to the fourteenth centuries C.E. A great Islamic civilization flourished, with superb achievements in art, science, literature, and scholarship.

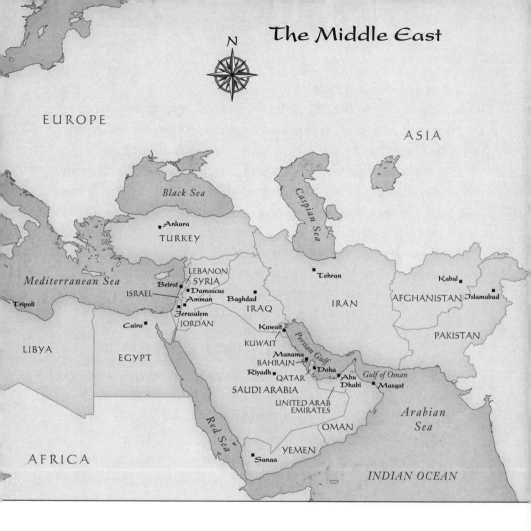

The Middle East

N

EUROPE

ASIA

Black Sea

Caspian Sea

Ankara
TURKEY

Mediterranean Sea

LEBANON
SYRIA
Beirut
Damascus
ISRAEL
Amman
Baghdad
Jerusalem
JORDAN
IRAQ

Tehran

Kabul

AFGHANISTAN Islamabad

IRAN

PAKISTAN

Tripoli

Cairo

Kuwait

KUWAIT

Manama
BAHRAIN
Riyadh
QATAR
Doha
Abu
Dhabi
Gulf of Oman
Masqat

LIBYA

EGYPT

Persian Gulf

SAUDI ARABIA

UNITED ARAB
EMIRATES

Arabian
Sea

OMAN

Red Sea

YEMEN
Sanaa

AFRICA

INDIAN OCEAN

As the golden age of Islam declined, European fortunes rose. The Western powers, especially France and England, gradually came to wield heavy control over the once proud Middle East.

In the nineteenth century, European involvement brought material benefits, such as improved health care and modern education. Yet it also resulted in deep resentment because the Europeans disrupted the existing societies and dominated them politically. In the mid-twentieth century, several Middle Eastern countries made intensive efforts to throw off European control. The scars from these battles are still felt. Many people also feel anger toward the United States for supporting Israel excessively, as they consider Israel an intrusive and unfriendly neighbor. Culturally and economically, too, the West is viewed with suspicion. The failure of Western-style economic systems to deliver hoped-for prosperity has brought disillusionment and frustration.

Only through understanding Middle Eastern history can we comprehend modern-day Arab resentment toward the West. Today, decades after independence from direct European rule, the Arab/Muslim encounter with the West still evokes feelings of both attraction and rejection. While many people desire what the West has to offer, others prefer a distinct and separate identity.

Modernization and Change

Whether welcome or not, change is already well under way in the Middle East. A guarantee of change is the rapid growth of urbanization, transforming the region from a land of villages and small towns to one with sprawling cities, which greatly

increases the impact of modernization. Even now, in the most remote corners of the area, aspects of Western culture from television and Pepsi to the effects of globalization affect people's lives and bring about social changes.

One result is tension between the traditional view of women and the role of women in a modern society. Women have been expected to submerge their

Bold style in Damascus

own identities and needs in the interest of the family, remaining at home to look after the men and children. This is a hallmark of patriarchal society, which can be described as one in which men are supreme, setting the values and maintaining control. In patriarchal society there may be a complementary relationship—men do one kind of work, women another, and both are valued—but too often the balance tips heavily in men's favor and women are kept in a second-class status. Middle Eastern societies are regarded as among the most patriarchal in the world.

Yet today most Middle Eastern women no longer automatically remain at home. Education and economic need have pushed increasing numbers into the workplace. This

A soldier in Libya

shift in women's roles has induced some men to readjust their expectations of women, while others feel threatened and want to force women back into their more traditional roles. The result is an intense political and social struggle, in which women are claiming an increasingly significant role.

Anthropologists remind us that societies are never monolithic—a uniform whole—but complex and changing. Thus we must keep in mind the great diversity in the region, even though most of the people share a common religion and culture. Middle Eastern women live in villages, deserts, and modern cities; some survive on next to nothing, while others lead lives of incredible luxury. Naturally their outlooks on life vary accordingly. While we cannot possibly depict in this book the infinite variety of women's lives, we can try to present some fairly typical situations and voices.

A Further Note on Definitions

Geographically, this book covers the following: the Levantine states of Lebanon, Syria, and Jordan, plus Iraq; the Arabian Peninsula and Persian Gulf states of Saudi Arabia, Yemen, Oman, Qatar, Bahrain, Kuwait, and the United Arab Emirates; and the North African states of Morocco, Algeria, Tunisia, Libya, and Egypt.

Although not part of the Arab world because of differences in language, history, and culture, Iran is also included in our survey. Its strong Islamic tradition, intimate connection with the Arab world, and influential role in regional politics make it an important part of any discussion of Middle

Eastern women. Similarly, Turkey—with a non-Arab but mostly Muslim population—will also be referred to occasionally. Because of Turkey's proximity to the Arab countries and its long rule over those countries as the Ottoman Empire (from the fifteenth to the early twentieth century), it is an intrinsic part of the Middle East in many ways.

Although the political future of the Palestinian people is not settled, they are very much a vital Middle Eastern population. An Arab people who lived for many centuries in the land that is now Israel, they now inhabit areas called the West Bank and Gaza. There are also Palestinians living in Israel and, mostly as refugees, in neighboring Arab states.

The state of Israel, however, as a recent creation of unique historic forces, is not included in this discussion. Because of the predominantly European roots of its culture, Israeli society remains distinct from its Arab neighbors. Typically, Israeli women lead lives more like those of Europeans and Americans than those of Arab women. Nonetheless, we can envision closer cultural and social links between Israelis and Arabs sometime in the future.

Finally, this new edition of our book includes a chapter specifically on Afghanistan. While Afghanistan usually is not considered a Middle Eastern country, it shares the religion of Islam and some cultural similarities. Moreover, because recent political and military events have drawn American attention to Afghanistan so intensely, and because these developments inevitably have an impact on Iran and the Arab states, we consider it relevant to include a brief explanation of what has been happening to women in Afghanistan.

2

Growing Up

Every daughter is a handful of trouble.

—Arab proverb

Flowers break rocks.

—Tunisian proverb

*M*iddle Eastern families dote on children. Proverbs express this love—"A house without a child is like a house without a light" —and the Prophet Muhammad encouraged kind treatment of girls. Yet in Middle Eastern cultures the celebration of a little boy's birth is typically a good deal livelier than that for a girl, and most wives feel tremendous pressure to produce sons. Why is there such a strong preference?

In farming communities there are practical reasons: although girls work at least as hard, sons are valued for the muscle power they can provide in the fields. In both urban and rural societies sons are expected to provide for their aging parents. Sons may also work in the city or a foreign land and send money home. But girls are seen by traditional families more as an expense than a benefit, since at marriage they leave home to live with—and work for—the husband's family.

A man is typically known by his first son's name—for instance, "father of Najeeb," Abu Najeeb. The baby's mother becomes Um Najeeb, "mother of Najeeb." Some parents take the name of a daughter who is firstborn, but a son's name is far more common.

Girls' names usually have attractive meanings. For instance, Amal means "hope," and Rima, "gazelle"; Jameela means "beautiful," and Laila, "evening." In Tunisia, however, the feminine name Dalenda is supposed to ensure that a mother's next baby will be a boy. The explanation comes from ancient times when the powerful empire of Carthage (Tunisia) fought against Rome. The Roman war cry *"Delenda est Carthago!"* (Carthage must be destroyed) was preserved in folk tradition, and Dalenda came to be used as a name to "destroy" the likelihood of any more daughters.[1]

Children at Siwa, an oasis in the western desert of Egypt

A Girl's Early Years

Despite a preference for sons, it's often a young daughter who becomes the father's darling. Affection between children and relatives starts with all the hugging that babies get. In some families a young girl is taught to kiss the cheek of a woman to whom she has just been introduced, and the custom of cheek kissing continues among friends throughout life.

At home girls are generally expected to do more than boys. They begin running errands at an early age, washing dishes, preparing food, and taking charge of younger children. It's not uncommon in rural communities to see a child of five carrying a baby on her back. In such countries as Lebanon, Jordan, and Kuwait, in contrast, child rearing has taken a markedly different and problematic turn. There, well-to-do families often have servants—usually from Sri Lanka or the Philippines—to look after their children. The mother is freed for her own pursuits, while the children are being brought up by a woman from a very different culture and possibly missing out on some of their own cultural values and behavior patterns.

Before puberty, girls enjoy considerable equality with boys. They can usually run about freely, in some countries even entering the mosque where the men are praying. Scouting is popular from elementary to high school, and sometimes the troops are mixed, girls and boys together. In liberal societies, such as Lebanon and Tunisia, young girls and boys play and participate in activities together as much as in Western countries. But they probably will not have as many toys, which are expensive.

One Western toy, the Barbie doll, has proved both irresistible and controversial. When Barbie—with her bosom, bikini, and worst of all, boyfriend—drew protests, more suitable dolls were created in Egypt and Iran. "Laila" and "Sara"

At a community day care center in Tripoli, Libya, young girls and boys play together.

look about ten or twelve years of age, reflect the coloring and clothing of young Egyptians and Iranians, and have brothers, not boyfriends. But such is the cultural conflict in many Middle Eastern societies that blond Barbie—and all she represents of Western values—still has allure.[2]

To an unfortunate degree, television and computer games fill the leisure hours of most young people in urban areas. But some children have little leisure at all, for example those employed in the carpet-making industries of Iran and Egypt. The tying of tiny knots in "Persian carpets" requires small, nimble fingers, and girls as young as eight may spend long hours sitting at looms.

The First Change of Life

Life begins to change for a girl in a conservative Middle Eastern family when she reaches the age of ten or eleven. Her mother prepares her for her role as a woman, teaching traditional feminine behavior and skills. She will dress modestly, speak quietly, and mix less freely with boys. As her brothers begin to assert their authority she learns to obey and not talk back.

An anthropologist in a Moroccan town observed: "One little girl in particular comes to mind; at six she was almost as much of a tease as her brother, with a twinkle in her eye and a ready laugh. But by ten she had become more restrained, and by twelve she was a 'perfect little lady,' seldom running or giggling, and the sparkle was replaced by a soberness and a sense of responsibility."[3]

This transformation into a "little woman" takes many forms. In a Bedouin community a girl learns the skills of the nomadic life—spinning wool, weaving, cooking, collecting firewood, tending the goat herd. In poor families girls may be pulled out of school to devote themselves to housework, while the boys continue their education. In the city a middle-class girl learns hostessing skills early. When guests arrive, she helps her mother serve them fruits, sweets, and drinks, then sits patiently until dismissed. By adolescence most girls in the Middle East have learned the importance of recognizing the bounds of proper female behavior.

What is so significant about puberty is that a girl in a conservative community must radically change her behavior and her outlook on life, becoming burdened with restrictions that don't apply to the boys? A simple fact of life: her family feels they must now protect her both from the attentions of men and from her own sexual awakening. Childhood ends early and abruptly for many young girls.

A young girl in Yemen begins learning skills that will carry into adulthood.

Chapter 3

School Days

More precious than the blood of martyrs is the ink of scholars.
—Arab proverb

*I*f a girl will spend her life cooking and having babies, why does she need to read or write? This was a common attitude in much of the Middle East until the last fifty years or so.

Girls study the Qur'an in Yemen.

Yet learning is highly valued in Islam. The holy book of Islam, the Qur'an, says, "The seeking of knowledge is a duty of every Muslim man and every Muslim woman." During the golden age of Islamic civilization, women were not left out. Yemen, for example, boasted prominent female poets and legal scholars, and Muslim women in many places practiced as trained doctors.[1]

As Islamic civilization declined from the fourteenth century through the nineteenth, however, so did schooling. Boys went to traditional religious schools, where they did little more than memorize the Qur'an. Girls generally learned only household skills and crafts.

Modern Education

In the early nineteenth century idealistic American missionaries started going to Lebanon and Palestine, where the populations included many Christians who belonged to indigenous churches. Rather than try to change people's religion, the missionaries wisely focused on schooling and gave particular attention to the education of girls.[2]

By the middle of the nineteenth century, religious and philanthropic groups from the United States, France, Britain, and other European countries were opening schools in Syria, Egypt, and Turkey. Upper-class families in Turkey hired European governesses, and a secondary school for girls was started in 1858.

Progressive Muslim organizations, especially in Lebanon, joined this movement in the 1870s and established their own schools for both girls and boys. In Egypt some liberal thinkers stressed education of girls as an important step in strengthening Muslim society.

Not everywhere, however, was modern education welcomed. In Algeria, which had been seized by France in the 1830s, the colonial rulers tried to establish schools like those in France, while suppressing the indigenous people and their culture. The Algerians found French education alien and inappropriate, and very few families sent their daughters to school.[3]

For the first half of the twentieth century, education in the Middle East was available only for the well-to-do residing in urban areas. Lebanon was the exception; there, especially in the Christian areas, almost every village had a primary school and most girls attended for at least a few years. The great majority of children elsewhere went without modern schooling. Conservative families, claiming that Islam held all knowledge, argued that a girl who could read and write would communicate secretly with someone outside her home. Besides, money spent on her schooling would be wasted when she went to live with her husband's family.

Governments began to play a much larger role in public education after World War II. In the oil-rich but isolated Gulf states, from the 1960s on, comparatively progressive rulers used some of their wealth for social programs. Schooling was free, and even in conservative places, people accepted the view that educating daughters was socially proper and not contrary to their religious beliefs.[4]

Today the principle of universal education is established in virtually all countries of the Middle East and North Africa. Only where a poor country's resources are stretched too thin by a rapidly increasing population, as in Egypt, or in isolated communities that resist modern ideas, some children grow up without any schooling.

How Many Girls in School?

Numbers do not tell us everything, and reliable figures are not readily available. They suggest, however, that Middle Eastern girls have *almost* as good a chance at getting a basic education as do boys.

At the elementary level, girls make up about 45 to 50 percent of most countries' school enrollments. Only in Yemen are there still far fewer girls than boys in school. At the secondary level there is some drop-off, but not much. Typically, less than 50 percent of high school students are girls; in the Gulf states, Jordan, and Libya the percentage is a little higher. The required number of years of schooling differs from country to country: eight or nine is typical, while Tunisia requires eleven.[5]

Palestinians present a special case, for both political and cultural reasons. They have long placed high value on education; there were schools for girls in the latter part of the nineteenth century.[6] After the founding of Israel in 1948, which created great numbers of Palestinian refugees, schooling became partly an international responsibility, with United Nations schools in the refugee camps. Palestinians emphasize education—for both sexes—as the key to a better future, and are among the best educated of all the Arab peoples.

Off to School—A Few Examples

Although Lebanon has fairly good public schools throughout the country, most families prefer to send their daughters and sons to private schools if they can afford it. The majority of schools are for both sexes through all the grades, with some well-known schools for girls only. Because both private and public schools emphasize foreign languages, French and English, most schoolchildren learn at least one foreign language fluently in addition to their native Arabic. Discipline is firm, especially at the many schools run by Lebanese Catholic nuns.

In Egypt, like Lebanon, any family who can possibly afford it is likely to choose a private school. The expense is beyond crowded and have little room for recreation. After age eleven or twelve, most girls and boys attend separate schools.

The long walk to school in southern Jordan

Public schools are overcrowded, often running in two shifts. Even here, education is not cheap. To prepare for exams, students at both public and private schools usually have to arrange tutoring lessons with their teachers. The teachers, a large percentage of whom are women and very poorly paid, depend on this extra income. For poor families this added expense is an almost impossible burden, which doubtless raises the question, in many homes, of whether a daughter's schooling is as important as her brother's.

In Saudi Arabia the "two societies"—male and female—require separate schools from kindergarten through university. Students learn primarily in Arabic but start a foreign language, usually English, in the early grades; this is true throughout the Middle East. A Saudi girl is usually driven to school by her family's chauffeur, bright and early: school starts at 7 A.M. and finishes in the early afternoon because of the heat. She wears a long-sleeved blouse and an ankle-length skirt, her hair in a ponytail with a black ribbon. When she reaches seventh grade, she has to wear an *abbayah* (full-length black cloak) to and from school.

At the other extreme is Tunisia. Classes, taught in both Arabic and French, include both sexes. When school lets out in the afternoon, girls and boys in jeans and denim jackets chat together very much like students at an American high school. To make secondary school accessible to more young people, the competitive entrance exams were abolished in 1994.

School in the Middle East is not designed to be fun. Everywhere, it is a serious business. Teaching methods are apt to be old-fashioned and uninspiring, focused on preparing students for exams. In Egypt, for example, even children in the earliest grades must take long final examinations. Students learn to store up facts rather than explore ideas, and except at the best schools, there's little time for such "frills" as art, music, and sports.

Books and other educational materials convey stereotypical roles—women as mothers and teachers, men in more varied activities. Fortunately, some educators are aware of the need for change; Libya, for example, is producing textbooks that counter negative stereotypes of women.[7] Significant progress in reducing gender bias, however, may be slow in coming. For one thing, publishers in Lebanon produce children's books for the whole region and have to cater to the views of educational authorities in the Gulf states. Thus conservative attitudes in the Arabian Peninsula tend to set standards for a much wider area.[8]

Until the last few years, children's books produced in the Middle East have mostly been moralistic tales, usually set in the "Arabian Nights" past. Reading material aimed specifically at girls, which would meet their interests and expand their horizons, is rare. Imported books are generally too expensive for most families. Little by little, however, children's literature is improving. An organization in Kuwait has undertaken an ambitious publishing program, including books that deal with subjects of concern to young people, such as war, death, sex, and the environment. Typically, however, children associate books with school only. They don't think of reading for fun and interest, especially wherever television and the Internet beckon.[9]

Serious and capable girls whose families have been able to send them to good schools will likely wind up with an excellent academic education. Although in traditional societies it's usually the mother who most vigorously backs education for her daughters, many women give credit for their success in life to supportive, farsighted fathers.

Girls at this private school in Cairo wear uniforms—but the long skirts are a fashion choice, not a requirement.

Higher Education

Some girls head for universities in Europe and the United States, while others go to private or national universities in their own countries. The American University of Beirut, foremost in modern education in the region, started accepting girls in 1924. Cairo University followed in 1927, and the University of Damascus admitted women in 1941. In most other countries, coeducation at the university level has been much more recent.

Higher education of women has made huge strides in most of the conservative Arabian and Gulf states. In Kuwait, where the oil industry brought dramatic changes almost overnight, women students entered the University of Kuwait as soon as it opened in 1966 and in eight years made up about 60 percent of the enrollment.

Saudi Arabia started public education for girls in 1960 and admitted the first female students to a university around 1965. Although facilities are up-to-date, education is strictly segregated. Women students see their male professors only on closed-circuit television screens. At first Saudi women students were educated only for occupations that served women, such as teaching and medicine. Women started going abroad to study in 1979 and now pursue a wide range of career possibilities.

In Bahrain, an oil-rich island nation, the government realized the need to develop women's talents quickly, to reduce dependence on foreign expertise. By the mid-1960s there were equal numbers of schools for girls and boys in the towns, and women students were being sent to universities in other countries.[10]

Iran, aiming to build an economically strong Islamic society, encourages women to go into nearly every field. Female and male university students are about equal. An Iranian woman in the United States who visits her country periodically describes the young women students thus:

Top: High school students after class in Tunis
Bottom: A campus scene at the American University of Beirut, Lebanon

"They are vibrating with life, thirsty for knowledge. They can't wait to learn and to do things—the way my mother's generation felt when coming out from under the veil."[11]

Entrance to universities is extremely competitive. Today the best women students can hope for good academic preparation in whatever field they choose. Although the majority prefer liberal arts, law, and education, many go into science, medicine, and engineering more than in the United States. In Libya, 64 percent of medical and engineering students are women. Furthermore, at both secondary and university levels, girls do noticeably better than boys. This may be because many superior male students go abroad to study, but also because female students are motivated and serious.

In the Gulf states today, women university students significantly outnumber males, and this has brought social problems. The ever-increasing numbers of well-educated female graduates have trouble finding both jobs and husbands. According to a United Nations specialist in that region, many men don't want wives with a better education than they have.[12]

Opportunities are improving for teacher training and vocational education, particularly commercial, but this type of education lags far behind the university in availability and prestige. The idea that an "educated person"—regardless of sex—is almost necessarily a doctor, lawyer, engineer, or professor is still strong in the Middle East.

Literacy

Many of the mothers—certainly the grandmothers—of the present generation of students have a different story. They probably grew up before public schooling became widespread in their area, or during times of war, or in impoverished or conservative communities. Typically, women who missed out on schooling want their daughters and granddaughters to have better chances so that they can "learn and do different things from what we have to do, and defend their rights."[13]

Of the female population who were over age fifteen in the mid-1990s, the proportion who are literate ranges from 80 percent for Palestinians and Lebanese to about 25 percent for Yemenis. Not surprisingly, many more women than men cannot read and write: for instance, 50 percent of women in Egypt compared with 33 percent of men, and in Morocco, 64 percent of women compared with 38 percent of men.[14] These figures include rural and nomadic populations, in which the great majority of women are illiterate.

The good news is that the gap between women and men is getting steadily smaller. Literacy programs target women, and the percentage of women who can read and write is definitely increasing. An innovative program run by a woman in Algeria, called "*Iqraa!*" (Read!), reaches tens of thousands of rural women, with support from local religious leaders.[15]

A woman's literacy class in Jordan

But resistance to educating girls is still entrenched in some places. In parts of Yemen parents will not let their daughters attend school with boys or even walk through the streets to the school.[16] Recent Peace Corps workers in Morocco—a country with wide disparities between its elite class of educated women and its numerous illiterate rural women—were discouraged by village attitudes. "I tried to start a literacy program in my villages," reported one young woman. "The women wanted it, the girls pleaded for it, and for two years we fought for it. In the end, the men stopped it. They were illiterate, too, and there was no way they were going to let their already strong women get the upper hand." [17]

The education of girls raises social and personal questions about its value. The social issue has to do with population growth. In developing countries, education of women has been found essential in all efforts to lower the birthrate and improve the quality of life. Middle Eastern and North African states, with their high rates of population growth, therefore have a major stake in providing good schooling for all classes of girls—especially the poorer, who are most likely to have large families.

As for the personal factor, arguments for girls' education primarily emphasize that it will benefit families and society. Much less noted is the idea of developing girls' minds and abilities for their own fulfillment as individuals. Surely that's an attitude ripe for change.

While living in Cairo a few years ago, the author (EM) often chatted with a beggar girl of about twelve, a sassy, feisty kid who sat every day on a curb near a luxury hotel. One day I asked whether she would like to go to school. "How I wish it!" she answered fervently in Arabic. "How I wish it!"

Doubtless she is now married and a mother. But maybe her daughters or granddaughters will have better chances.

4

Religion and Tradition

God has omitted women from his mercy.

—Arabic proverb

The believers, men and women, are protectors one of another; on them will Allah pour his mercy.

—Holy Qur'an, sura 9: 71–72

Although education is critically important to young women today, another force may ultimately play an even larger role in their lives. In the Middle East, religion—the beliefs and institutions that help define people's ideas about God, humanity, and society—has a great deal to say about women's behavior.

Many Religions, Varied and Vital

While the Middle East is generally associated with the Islamic faith, it also holds a fascinating mix of other religious traditions. Christianity is an important presence in the region. In Egypt, somewhere between 6 and 10 percent of the population is Coptic Christian. The Levantine countries, especially Lebanon, Syria, and Palestine include important Maronite, Orthodox, and Roman Catholic Christian communities, most of which go back to the first and second centuries. In addition, there are small Protestant groups.

Women pray at a mosque in Baghdad.

Religion in the Middle East is not just about private faith but is an all-encompassing way of seeing the world, concerned with how society should be run as much as with personal belief and morality.

Long ago, religious leaders set up strong behavioral guidelines, especially for relations between the sexes. Without these rules, it was feared, people would forget about God and important values of honor, family loyalty, and proper behavior. The result would be something like the godless ways that to many religious people in the Arab/Muslim world characterize the West today.

Religion can give people a purpose and a strong sense of identity, yet it may also restrict personal freedom. In religions developed and led by men, as all Middle Eastern religions are, this burden falls most heavily on women. These patriarchal religions, notably Islam, consider it important for the well-being of society that women remain primarily wives and mothers, supporting their families and asking little for themselves. But as we shall see, women have ways to get around restrictions and make their lives more tolerable. Just as important, most Middle Eastern women believe their roles as wives and mothers offer valuable positive identities.

Islam

Islam began in seventh-century Arabia with the teachings of the Prophet Muhammad.

Muslims believe that Muhammad received revelations from God (*Allah* in the Arabic language), telling him how the individual and society should behave in order to be faithful to the one true God—the God of the Hebrew and Christian Bible. Building on the Jewish and Christian scriptural beliefs, Islam called on men and women everywhere to forsake false idols and worship God alone. Muhammad's revelations were recorded in the Islamic holy book, the Qur'an. Accounts of the Prophet's actions and sayings, called the Hadith, also became an important part of the Islamic tradition.

The basic beliefs of Islam are that there is only one God, and Muhammad is God's final messenger in a long succession of prophets. It is in the practice of Islam—the way Muslims express their faith—that this religion's power becomes apparent. Muslims must follow certain requirements, called the Five Pillars of Islam, which are simple and direct. They are the sincere statement of faith in God, prayer five times a day, almsgiving to the poor, fasting during the month of Ramadan, and a pilgrimage to the holy city of Mecca in Saudi Arabia if at all possible. Muslims are expected to serve God not only by living pure and modest lives but also by working for social justice. The Qur'an emphasizes good treatment of the poor and unfortunate, while denouncing dishonesty, bribery, and greed.

In the Five Pillars we see the purest expression of Muhammad's bold revelation that all persons are equal in the eyes of God. Men and women of all classes, races, and nationalities are called upon to make the same commitment and share the same spiritual rewards.

Pilgrimage, Ramadan, and Prayer

Probably the greatest religious experience for any Muslim is the pilgrimage. Each year millions of Muslims travel to Mecca to worship at the Ka'ba, the most sacred shrine in Islam. Women from all over the Muslim world make this difficult journey and find it a tremendously rewarding experience. It may well be the only glimpse they get of the spiritual equality of the sexes that Muhammad said God intended. Whereas in their own homes and societies they may suffer glaring inequality, at Mecca they mix as equals with all believers, male and female. The pilgrimage can also be an eye-opening social experience for them as they share life stories with women from every land.

Another activity much loved by Muslim women, especially in Egypt, North Africa, and Iran, is pilgrimage to the shrines of Muslim saints. A shrine is one of the few places where women in traditional societies can gather without disapproval. There they can pray, make requests of the saints, or simply visit in a woman-friendly place.

The fourth Pillar, fasting during the Islamic month of Ramadan, is another positive spiritual experience. For a full month, women and men alike (unless their health forbids it) are not supposed to eat or drink anything from dawn to dusk. This form of self-discipline is an expression of repentance for sins and a reminder of the Muslim's dependence on God for all things. Every day it ends with a joyous and plentiful fast-breaking meal, called the *iftar*, that the women of the family have prepared.

At first glance, prayer appears to be one Pillar in which the sexes are not so equal. One sees many more men than women at prayer in mosques, and the women pray in a separate room. Yet the explanation for this makes sense: separating women from men allows each group to go through the physical motions of praying (kneeling, bending, bowing toward Mecca) without being touched or stared at by the opposite sex. Worshippers are thus freed from distraction.

Women can pray at home for the sake of both modesty and their small children. Yet women are increasingly claiming their place at the mosque. In such cities as Cairo and Tehran, women have organized study and prayer groups at their local mosques. Here they can take active leadership roles in a setting otherwise dominated by men.

Throughout the Middle East, popular culture combines "official" religion with folk beliefs and local superstitions. In North Africa, women known as *shawafas* are believed able to communicate with saints, and women often visit a shawafa to seek help with personal matters such as infertility or marital problems. Similarly, there is widespread belief in the "evil eye," a mysterious malevolent force to be warded off by blue amulets and frequent mention of God's name. Women in traditional societies often set store by such supernatural attempts to improve their families' fortunes.

The Problem of Inequality in Islamic Societies

Muhammad's emphasis on respect for women produced other improvements intended to protect women and enhance their position in society.[1] For instance, women were given the rights to receive education, earn income, inherit property, and manage their own property, along with the right to initiate divorce under certain circumstances. Indeed, many of the legal reforms that Muhammad instituted in seventh-century Arabia did not appear in Western societies until well into the nineteenth century.

One feature of Islam considered backward by many people in the West was in fact instituted to protect women. In pre-Islamic society, men could marry as many women as they pleased. Muhammad announced a revelation that a Muslim man could have no more than four wives at the same time—and, even then, only if he could support and treat them all equally.

Yet deep inequalities do exist in Muslim society, which go back to the great diversity of religious belief in the Middle East. Wherever Islam took hold, historically it mixed with local customs and beliefs. The result has been a variety of "Islams," with differing beliefs about women.

A distinction must be made between *modernist* Muslims, who argue that genuine Islam is compatible with the modern values of science, democracy, and equal rights, and *conservative* Muslims, who prefer a more traditional and patriarchal society based on strictly Islamic ideas. Both groups claim that their views on the place of women are supported

Women gather for prayer at a mosque in Cairo.

by the Qur'an plus Muhammad's teachings. Like other complex religious literature, the Qur'an can be interpreted in differing ways. On one hand, it encourages men to treat women with respect, justice, and sensitivity. Yet it contains many reminders of the male-dominated culture that Muhammad lived in: "Men have a status above women," and "Men have authority over women because God has made one superior to the other."[2]

Moreover, many of the later Islamic leaders interpreted the Qur'an and the early Islamic law codes to support the existing male biases in their societies. The result, over the centuries, has been a religious, legal, and social system much less friendly to women than Muhammad probably would have wished.

Those who defend Islam as a positive force for women tend to emphasize the rights promoted by Muhammad and his example as a good husband. Those who consider it an oppressive system for women tend to look at the gap between the Islamic ideal and the reality. In marriage arrangements, for example, the Qur'an indicates a woman's right to contract her own marriage, but a conservative father can overrule that right. Muhammad discouraged divorce and tried to protect wives, yet religious judges soon devised ways to allow men to divorce their wives easily.

Women Seen as a Danger

There are deeper reasons for the lack of freedom that women experience in conservative Muslim societies. A woman's behavior is regarded as basic to the well-being of society itself.

Too much freedom for women, conservative Muslims argue, threatens the stability of family and society. A good woman obeys her husband and avoids other men. Unveiled women, and those who seek to make their own choices about marriage, are violating God's rules for a good society.

At the base of this view is the idea that women are by definition seductive creatures too attractive for men to resist. Thus, women can lead men to loss of self-control and, ultimately, the breakdown of orderly Islamic society. Barriers between the sexes must therefore be maintained.[3] Keeping a woman indoors is the best guarantee; but if she must go out, she should cover herself with a "curtain of modesty" to conceal her attractiveness. Free from sexual distractions, men can thus focus more attentively on their proper responsibilities toward God, family, and society. Many conservative Muslims point to the greater freedom of women in the West as the prime cause of undesirable behavior patterns—such as frequent divorce, abortion, and adultery—that they see as rampant in Western society.

Rise of Islamism

Among conservatives, a strong movement has been developing in the last half century that calls for revival of society based on strictly religious values and beliefs. Generally termed *Islamism*, this Islamic revival is also often referred to as *Islamic fundamentalism*. In general, fundamentalists—who are found in all religions—believe that the sacred writings of their religion must be taken literally and that religion must be restored to what they consider its early, uncorrupted ideals and practices. They believe that society and law must be organized according to these narrowly interpreted religious "fundamentals."

Many experts on Islam, however, point out that the ideas preached by so-called Islamic fundamentalists often do not represent the true beliefs and values of Islam, and may even be serious distortions. Therefore, they feel, the term *Islamism* is preferable to *Islamic fundamentalism*, and that's what we shall use here.

The rapid growth of Islamism in the Middle East has been fed largely by a widespread mood of desperation. The economies of many countries are in bad straits. Political problems, such as the long-standing Palestinian-Israeli conflict and the dangerous regime in Iraq, keep people in a constant state of anxiety and anger. Many people are losing faith in their governments' power to solve basic social and economic problems.

Islamists, therefore, wish to revitalize the Muslim world and solve its many problems through strictly Islamic principles. Waging a campaign to rid their societies of Western influence, which they see as a threat to Muslim values, they call for strict enforcement of Islamic law, the *shari'a*, and have little tolerance for dissent or difference.

The growth of Islamism is perhaps the most troubling development for women in the Middle East today, because Islamists focus a great deal on the place of women in society. One of the main goals of the more radical proponents is to return women to their "proper" place in the home. They argue that many of the problems of the Middle East result from the weakening of the traditional family and that independent women with Western ideas of sexual freedom and equality pose the greatest threat to family and society. A woman out earning money may cause trouble by encountering strange men in the workplace and is also usurping the role of the father in the family.

Islamist leaders encourage their followers to run conservative households in which wives are clearly subservient to their husbands. More threateningly, they also seek to change their countries' laws by imposing the strictest form of the shari'a on everyone.

In Iran, the shari'a was reinstated as the law of the land in 1979, after years of Western-influenced law. The government eventually modified its policies, but it still tries to enforce Islamic ideals. Saudi Arabia, with its own form of ultraconservative Islamic rule, has a special "morality police," who aggressively watch for such offenses as women driving cars or unmarried couples appearing together in public.

Today's Islamism is largely an urban movement. At heart, Islamism is a reaction against disturbing change, and change is nowhere more apparent or disturbing than in the large Middle Eastern city. Young men who have recently moved to the city are often shocked by the more liberal behavior of city women. They also feel threatened by the thought of competing with women for jobs. These bewildered youths often turn to Islamism, with its emphasis on restoring "proper" gender relations and combating Western influence in government. In Islamism they find a way both to reassert traditional male authority and to seek an explanation for the social chaos they see in the modern city.

Women's Responses to Islamism

Islamist movements appeal to some women, who organize women's subgroups. The Iranian revolution, for instance, had the active support of many women. A Palestinian Islamist group called the Muslim Sisters argues that genuine Islam offers positive, empowering roles for women. Their own self-confident example as they teach and work for social change has won admiration among other Palestinian women.[4]

From Iran to Morocco, increasing numbers of people are learning to discuss religious questions intelligently, rather than just listening to the authorities.[5] Traditionally, only men could study religion, especially at the higher institutions of Islamic learning. But women are no longer willing to let men be the only ones who study and interpret the Qur'an and shari'a. Now women are educating themselves on all points of their religion and developing their own interpretations, often in the face of prevailing conservative opinion. As one Iranian women put it, "The *mullahs* [religious authorities] are trying to use the Qur'an against us, but we have a surprise for them: we're going to beat them at their own game."[6]

Christianity

So far we have looked mainly at Islam. Other religious groups share some of the conservative thinking of Islam, but also have their own distinctive attitudes toward women. For centuries Christians—some sects more than others—have tended to look partly to the West for their values and religious connections. Even so, the laws and attitudes of the various Christian sects put women in a decidedly inferior position.

Yet Christian women are becoming more assertive. Along with the charitable activities that have always been the female role in the church, women are now obtaining greater power in decision-making bodies. They can be successful scholars and teachers of religion and are often involved in the running of retreats and religious conferences.

On the whole, the age-old traditions and patriarchal religions of Middle Eastern society act as constant reminders that it is men who are ultimately in charge. Religion, then, affects women's lives ambivalently. It provides them with spiritual inspiration and social identity— yet it also serves as the "divinely ordained" justification for men's efforts to remain dominant.

5

Becoming a Wife

*Marry off your daughter and remove the
shame from your house.*
—Iraqi proverb

*He who has the money can have the Sultan's
daughter for his bride.*
—Arabic proverb

arriage is still the central fact in the lives of most Middle Eastern women, partly because it is viewed as the normal, healthy way to live. Arab/Muslim societies strongly endorse modest, conservative family lives, a value explicitly encouraged by Islam.

Virtue, Reputation, and Honor

Just as important, however, is the notion of family honor. Customarily, the honor of the family depends on the behavior of its female members. Men's behavior is also governed by concepts of uprightness and shame, but the most essential guarantee of a traditional family's honor is the woman's virtue—meaning her sexual purity.

This attitude gave rise, in the patriarchal Middle East, to some interesting ideas about the nature of women. For example, an Arab proverb says, "He who has a daughter in the house has a fiery oven." The awakening of the girl's sexuality is regarded as a powerful, almost uncontrollable force. She must be closely watched, lest her runaway sexual appetite lead her into trouble.

Having a daughter "disgrace herself" would be one of the worst events imaginable, shaming the entire family. Her father and brothers, taking it as a matter of honor that they are responsible for her behavior, may insist on chaperoning her whenever she leaves the house. She may have to wear a concealing cloak and veil to protect her from the gaze of strangers and to tell the world that she is virtuous and unapproachable.

A conservative father may try to marry off his daughters by their midteens. This will free him from the burden of protecting their virginity and honor and, in financially pinched families, the expense of supporting them. One of the sad side effects of impoverished Palestinians' lives, both in refugee camps and in the midst of hostilities between Palestinians and Israelis, is that many girls are marrying very young to lessen the financial burden on their families.[1]

In general, however, the age of first marriage for women has been steadily rising, as a result of legal changes in some countries and education. It ranges from around twenty in Yemen to the late twenties in Lebanon and Libya. This tends to reduce the difference in age between wife and husband, now around five years on the average. But the longer young women wait to marry, the fewer the available men, especially in populations where many men emigrate to find work, such as Palestinians, Egyptians, and Yemenis.

Marriage as a Business Arrangement

In spite of the rich tradition of love poetry, not to mention romantic movies, the idea of marriage as the union of two people madly in love is still the exception rather than the rule. Love matches occur mainly in the educated middle and upper classes. More often, marriage is an alliance between families who may be less concerned with the couple's compatibility than with questions of status and reputation. "Will this union bring prestige and economic benefits to our family? Can our daughter make a higher match, or is this the best we can hope for?"

The art of arranging and negotiating marriages is a complex, time-honored tradition. As girls reach marriageable age, armies of aunts, mothers, and grandmothers go to work to find her a suitable husband. (The same is often true for young men!)

In rural societies and also among the urban poorer classes, matches are sometimes arranged between first cousins. Each family is well acquainted with the other, and economic resources stay within the family. The custom is declining, however, because of the disadvantages: a failed marriage makes trouble within the extended family, and the offspring of such genetically close unions may be born with congenital defects. A more common route these days is for women friends to arrange matches between their sons and daughters. This is preferable to marriage into a completely unknown family.

Occasionally a girl may have to marry a man she has never met, especially if there is a good deal of wealth or power at stake. Forced marriages, however, are increasingly uncommon. Sometimes a woman may accept an undesirable marriage mainly to escape from the heavy control of her family. At least she will have her own home and some independence, if not happiness.

Courtship

Dating, in the American and European style, is quite rare in the Middle East. Except in some urban societies, it is still taboo for a young man and woman to be alone together, especially indoors. As a Middle Eastern proverb has it, "When a man and a woman are alone together, Satan is the third person present."

Yet even in the strictest societies young people find ways to meet. At universities, girls join student groups where they can meet boys without raising suspicion. In Iran, young people hike into the hills around Tehran or head for the ski slopes for a chance to meet away from the eyes of the "morals police."[2] Young couples in Cairo sit close together on benches along the Nile in the evening, doubtless hoping not to be recognized by a neighbor or family friend. Western-style dating has been going on in Lebanon for decades, especially in liberal settings such as universities in Beirut. In Damascus, couples walk sedately on the street—but that demeanor may change inside a nightclub, for instance.[3]

Typically, urban middle-class people are coming to view dating, or at least social contacts before marriage, as less shameful than before. Many parents now accept that their children's happiness is at least as important as making the right match and take pride in a daughter who chooses an appropriate husband on her own. More and more, a Middle Eastern girl insists on her right of choice, balancing her own desires, her family's wishes, and her suitor's prospects.

The Bargaining Table

Once a proposal has been accepted, the real negotiations begin. Each family tries to make the best deal possible. If the couple will be moving to a new household, buying the furnishings becomes a major issue. Couples expect to start out with a well-furnished apartment, "down to the spices in the kitchen." In the words of Maha, an Egyptian scholar, "What you start married life with is 'what you are.' It reflects on your social standing."[4]

Finally a contract is signed between the families. Marriage can be seen as not so much the fulfillment of romantic dreams as a contract to start a new life.

In Muslim society the husband-to-be has to pay the bride's family a certain amount in money or goods known as the *mahr*, sometimes called "bride wealth." Part is paid before the wedding, and the rest later. Traditionally, the purpose of mahr was to give the wife some wealth of her own. It can also discourage divorce: if the husband divorces his wife, usually he must give her any remaining mahr he has held back. In some educated urban societies, the custom seems to be declining into a largely symbolic gesture.

The Big Day

The marriage ceremony varies from place to place and according to social status, but it is almost always a festive and colorful occasion. Part of the bride's preparation consists of painting designs on her hands and feet with henna, a natural red dye. From Morocco to Iraq, even sophisticated women follow the old custom of "henna day."

Traditional designs painted in henna on the hands of Saudi Arabian girls.

In the Gulf states and Saudi Arabia, marriage has become extravagantly expensive. The size of the typical mahr that fathers ask has soared, and for young men on a limited salary, this has become a major obstacle. Then comes the social requirement of an enormously costly wedding. Many families simply cannot afford to get their daughters and sons properly married off. The increasing number of young people who remain unmarried for this reason prompted the United Arab Emirates government to set up a "marriage fund" to help families in need. Now it's used by almost everyone, and most of it goes to pay for the wedding.[5]

Many well-to-do urban couples hold the celebration in a five-star hotel or at a fancy restaurant or club, the bride and groom dressed in Western-style garb—long white satin dress and black tuxedo. There are lots of traditional wedding foods and festivities—dancing, drumming, and singing well into the night. In Saudi Arabia, two parties take place, one for women and another for men.

Last-minute touches for a Lebanese bride.

In conservative villages, the wedding night "proof" of the bride's virginity traditionally assumes great importance, with wedding guests and family members awaiting the groom's report. If a husband finds that his bride is not a virgin, he may feel disgraced enough to break the marriage contract. Once this happens, it can be very difficult for a woman to make another match.

In a few urban societies, such as Beirut and Tunis, some young couples—often already engaged or going steady—do have premarital sexual relations, but secretively. The problem of children born out of wedlock is growing, especially in parts of North Africa, where society at large seems not yet ready to face this matter. A Peace Corps volunteer in Morocco reports that she was told again and again, "You are mistaken. There are no single mothers in Morocco."[6]

There are cracks, then, in the proclaimed values of "honor" and "female-chastity-above-everything." The fact remains that a good reputation is extremely important for a young woman. Middle Eastern society still holds decidedly negative views on extramarital relations—for women. For men, it's another matter.

"Honor" Carried to Extremes

In some cases, the role of woman as embodiment of her family's honor leads to a horrifying conclusion. "Honor crimes" are a lamentable aspect of traditional Middle Eastern society.

The term honor crime refers to the premeditated killing of a female member of a family, usually unmarried, who has had a sexual relationship outside of marriage or who is even suspected of it. The problem is particularly associated with Jordan, where an average of twenty to twenty-five such killings take place each year.[7] It also happens in other countries, including Lebanon, Iraq, and Turkey.

The victim's murderer is one of her male relatives, often a younger brother. Not only is this sort of murder considered necessary in some social settings, but the murderer is not considered guilty of anything bad—rather, he is considered a hero. He may go free, especially if just a boy, or receive a sentence of a few months. As one man explained, "I had to kill her to preserve the family's honor. Society imposes these rules on us, and I did it to please society."[8] In some families even the women appear to support the "rightness" of honor killing. However heartbroken, the mother states that her daughter has besmirched her family's honor and must pay the price.

How can such an act be understood? In the more conservative, usually rural, tribal societies of the Middle East, a man must exert total control over his family to be respected. A woman who acts on her own (even if coerced or seduced into it) is seen as flouting her "protector's" authority, which makes him lose face in his community. To reassert his authority and redeem his family's honor, such a man reasons, his only option is to punish her. Thus honor killing can take place not only when a young woman has misbehaved sexually but when she defies his determination to make her marry. The threat of honor killing naturally creates an atmosphere of great fear for young women.

Since the mid-1990s the problem of honor crimes has stirred up a storm of outrage, especially in Jordan. Women's groups have publicized it, and university students discuss it heatedly. Queen Rania has marched in demonstrations, while journalists expose incidents that doubtless would have received little attention in the recent past. The energetic leader of the campaign, Rana Husseini, refers to shari'a law to back up her argument that honor killing contradicts Islam.[9] In the spring of 2000 a petition to clamp down on honor crimes collected 15,000 signatures.

As a result of this pressure, in 2000 the Jordanian government amended the Penal Code somewhat, but the change has not been very effective. Murders committed in a "fit of fury" can still draw very light sentences.[10]

Opponents of honor crime, who are fighting deeply ingrained patterns of thinking, have their work cut out for them. Nonetheless, Jordan may one day offer a striking example of how citizens can organize to bring about significant social change.

When a Woman Stays Single

As we have seen, marriage is regarded as the normal—almost the required—way of life. A woman still single past thirty may often recall a proverb that says, "It's better to have a husband of wood than remain an old maid." In the more conservative societies, a single woman will be looked after by her male relatives so long as she preserves her honor. Such "protective custody" can be a mixed blessing. In a large household, she may become a cherished auntie to the children and a companion for the young married women—but also, possibly, something like a maid.

There are certainly exceptions to the "rule" that marriage is mandatory. A woman from a liberal family may decide to remain single. Especially in Lebanon, a few women have taken this route. Some pursue professional careers; others work selflessly in order to educate nieces and nephews.

Today, some well-educated young women speak of postponing marriage indefinitely. An attractive college senior from a Lebanese Muslim family told the author (EM), "If I marry, it will only be much later—after I'm well into my career. Several men have asked for me, but I tell my father I won't even meet them." A few may rule marriage out because they value their independence too much or fear that a husband might turn abusive.

These women recognize, of course, that their decision may alienate them from their societies. Moreover, almost never can they expect complete independence, because they will probably live with their families. As an assertive young Palestinian woman said, "I'd never go live by myself.... There'd be a big question mark over my head. People would begin to ask, 'What, her parents want no part of her?' I couldn't manage that."[11]

CHAPTER

6

Married Life

*Marriage is like a castle under siege: those outside want
to get in, those within want to get out.*

—Arabic proverb

A woman with a husband can spin the moon on her finger.

—Syrian proverb

With marriage, a woman begins a radically new phase of her life. Newlyweds who can afford it will probably begin their own household. When the couple has to move in with the husband's family, life can be difficult for a new bride, for she must adjust to a new setting, a new role, and, most of all, a mother-in-law. The husband's mother, a powerful figure, may firmly dominate the new daughter-in-law to make sure she pleases her husband and stays in line. On the other hand, the two may get along well, which can make a huge difference in the new wife's happiness.

Still, the man usually is king. He expects to wield authority, make the decisions, and have his needs met. The wife is expected to serve and obey without objection. Marital relations often suffer from this imbalance. Even women who normally have strong, assertive personalities may find their lives ruled by fear whenever the husband is around.[1]

57

A family in Egypt, including the husband's mother

Secluding a Wife, Sharing a Husband

In the minds of many traditional Middle Eastern men, a wife who works outside the home—or in the past, who even ventured out of her house—reflects poorly on the husband. As a husband's status improves, he is likely to demand that his wife remain at home, a way of boasting to the world that his wife can afford to spend all her time reclining indoors. The novels of Nobel Prize–winner Naguib Mahfouz describe this mentality in Egypt in the first half of the twentieth century. But most women these days, especially in cities and towns, expect much more freedom.

A more problematic aspect of married life is polygamy, or multiple marriages, another way a man can show the world how wealthy and powerful he is. The practice is quite rare today, partly because most educated men find the idea repugnant and partly because it's financially impractical.

Islam stipulates that each wife of a multiple marriage must be treated *equally*—a very difficult condition to meet.

Except possibly in isolated rural areas where two wives share the work and provide company for each other, Muslim women generally hate the idea of polygamy. It often occurs when the first wife has not been able to produce a son, so she feels doubly humiliated by her husband's marrying a second, "better" woman. Throughout the Middle East, women are becoming increasingly vocal in their resistance to the practice. Although the law differs from country to country,[2] growing numbers of women stipulate certain requirements in the marriage contract that discourage the husband from even thinking about taking a second wife. Tunisia, in fact, has outlawed polygamy since 1956.

A Jordanian man poses for a photograph with his three wives and his children.

Keeping Up Appearances, Keeping Company

Along with entrenched attitudes about honor, an obsession with public opinion is common in the Middle East: "What will people think?" Keeping up appearances, even if they conceal a different reality, is of great importance.

In Ali Ghalem's contemporary Algerian novel, *A Wife for My Son*, the young bride soon learns what is expected of her. Her husband orders, "We will go out and you will wear your veil. What is it you're looking for? To get insulted by men and even kids? Do you want me to be ridiculed?"[3]

Not every husband, however, is so concerned with an image of total control. Middle Eastern societies reveal a wide range of interaction between husband and wife. At one extreme, many wives in the modern societies of Lebanon and Tunisia, for instance, expect equality with their husbands. More and more, married couples in these societies expect to enjoy each other's company and do things together—jogging, theater, picnics, whatever—just like compatible couples in the West.

At the other extreme are certain traditional societies, often rural, where wives and husbands enjoy neither equality nor companionship. In some Egyptian villages, the husband treats his wife as a child, especially if she is young and uneducated. Because it would be considered shameful for a husband and wife to show affection toward one another, they both concentrate on their children.[4] In the Gulf state of Oman, it is customary that husbands and wives do not appear in public together. An Omani woman has a public role as a mother, but her role as wife is strictly private.[5] Among the remaining nomadic Bedouin families, the women live together in one part of the tent and the men in another.

Yet in other traditional settings, couples can enjoy close relationships. A village woman in Turkey recently described her marital relationship this way: "I worked with my husband in the fields. Sometimes he'd say to me 'Please come, stand by me, even if you don't work.... You give me strength that way.' My husband and I always gave each other morale. That's how we got along so well all these years."[6]

Somewhere between equality and unquestioned male supremacy are many urban, educated couples still governed by traditional views. The husband may expect to be waited on and fed a wonderful dinner, even though his wife, too, has had a full day's work outside the home. He probably feels supported by both tradition and religion, because the Qur'an states that men are in charge of women.

A woman and her children in a traditional Gulf society.

At the same time, wives can have subtle influence, leaving the man the appearance of being all-powerful. "Arab wives know how to get what they want and still make the husband feel he's in charge," says Maha, the Egyptian woman referred to earlier. Especially as they get older, women can exert a lot of power within the home. Once the husband has established his ultimate authority, he is likely to leave the day-to-day management and decision making to his wife. As an Iranian grandmother told the author (RH), her husband always made the big decisions—but consulted her the evening before.

Domestic Violence

Here, however, we must turn to an aspect of the marital relationship that has come into the open only in the last few years. It's a problem that afflicts all kinds of people in all countries: domestic abuse, a problem made all the worse by the hush-hush atmosphere surrounding it. The reason for discussing abuse at some length, like honor killing, is not so much to criticize as to recognize reality and the ways women are trying to deal with it.

The Qur'an says that if a wife is "rebellious," the husband should "admonish her, banish her to her couch, and strike her." One interpretation that finds favor with many Muslims is that a husband should strike his wife only as a last resort, if she fails to respond to either reason or "the silent treatment." Muhammad himself was known to criticize wife-beaters. Yet this Qur'anic verse does appear to sanction physical violence to some extent.

Domestic violence probably stems as much from patriarchal attitudes as it does from religious sanction, for wife-beating is certainly not restricted to Muslims. In a culture that encourages men to see women as subservient by nature, husbands may be emotionally unprepared to deal with a wife or daughter who expresses her own ideas and demands.

Abuse has always been a forbidden topic in Middle Eastern societies (as in the United States until quite recently). In some communities people are apt to consider it normal behavior, hardly worth discussing. Everywhere, most people would think it shameful for a woman to reveal that her husband had beaten her. It's a strictly personal matter they say. A woman who dares report a beating to the police, whether in liberal Lebanon or conservative Yemen, is not likely to get much attention from them.[7]

That situation, however, is starting to change. In some

A poster created by the Tunisian Association of Democratic Women advises, "Violence is a curse and silence is painful."

countries, women are calling public attention to the problem and trying to do something about it. Domestic violence is now openly discussed on television and radio in Lebanon. Since 1993 a support center has been operating in Tunis, where abused women can talk about their experiences and receive psychological and legal counseling. Groups in Algeria and Morocco also provide these services for abuse victims, as do centers in the West Bank and Jerusalem for Palestinian women.[8]

A "Women's Tribunal" at which women from several countries presented personal testimonies took place in Beirut in June 1995, giving rise to an organization called the Lebanese Council to Resist Violence Against Women. The LCRVAW sponsors conferences, offers legal help at little or no cost, and maintains four busy hotlines where women can seek advice or just a sympathetic ear. A shelter in Lebanon operated by nuns but open to people of all religions helps abused women and children while trying to enlighten the husbands. These are small steps, unthinkable five or ten years ago, but they are a start in dealing with this hitherto unmentionable problem.[9]

Divorce

Societies differ in their attitudes toward divorce. In Iraq, with a low divorce rate, it "just isn't done"; better an unhappy marriage, people seem to feel, than a divorce.[10] On the other hand, among Egyptians and Moroccans divorce is much more commonplace. Middle Eastern Christians, whose religious law strongly discourages divorce, have a very low separation rate. In general, the incidence of divorce in the Middle East has not shown a marked increase or decrease during the recent decades of rapid social change.[11]

Islam, it's often charged, allows a man to divorce his wife any time he wishes, and the wife just has to accept it. The truth, of course, is not that simple, for the ending of a marriage is definitely discouraged. For one thing, it means a break between two families, not just between two individuals. The couple and their families are supposed to follow a lengthy procedure involving mediation and repeated attempts at reconciliation.

Yet traditional Islamic law does give the man the exclusive right to file for divorce, with little or no justification required. This is still the case in staunchly conservative nations such as Saudi Arabia. Most other Middle Eastern societies, or states have revised the shari'a law somewhat, requiring the husband to show good cause and to pay alimony.

In addition, women are increasingly winning the right to initiate divorce. An Egyptian reform adopted in 2000 speeds divorce requested by the wife, provided she gives up claim to any money due her from her husband. A decision passed by the Iranian parliament allows a woman to divorce a husband who is sterile or drug addicted. And Iranian women are not timid in the divorce court. "Make yourself beautiful. Try to win him back," the judge kindly advised one woman. "I don't *want* him back!" she promply retorted.[12]

Still, the law remains decidedly unbalanced in most countries. In Syria, for instance, if a woman initiates divorce, her husband does not have to pay her alimony or any remaining mahr. Knowing this, a husband may try to make his wife so miserable that she will ask for a divorce regardless of her own prospective loss.[13]

Initiating divorce is usually a desperate measure for a woman. Unless she already has a full-time job or can rely indefinitely on her family, she will have little means of support. Wary of this possibility, many women buy as much gold jewelry as they can. Although men control family property, women are allowed to keep their jewelry, clothing, and inherited property. Gold, then, becomes a wife's insurance against divorce.

If divorced, a woman will generally move back into her father's or brother's household. The search for a new partner will then begin, for a woman without a husband can easily become an object of both pity and gossip. Furthermore, with the rising cost of living and scarcity of affordable housing, few families can shelter a divorced woman and her children for very long. On the other hand, some divorced women who can support themselves prefer to set up their own households and remain unmarried, especially in the cities.[14]

If the divorced couple has children, a court will usually decide who receives custody. Often the court automatically follows the shari'a law of custody, which states that the mother may have custody only until her children reach a certain age, usually around eight to twelve (each country is different). At that point the father or his family assume full responsibility. Even during the mother's custody, the father controls important decisions such as schooling and is supposed to pay child support. The rationale for this whole arrangement is that the children belong to the father's family, not the mother's. Also, since many men would not want to bring up another man's children, a woman without children may have more luck in finding a new husband.

In most Middle Eastern nations today, the trend is toward increased custody rights for the mother. Tunisian courts, for example, are instructed to decide cases in the best interests of the child, which often means full custody for the mother. Nonetheless, the fear of losing their children is another potent reason why many Middle Eastern women dread divorce.

Signs of Change

As women become educated and employed, many men are starting to see them as more than just wives, mothers, gracious hostesses, and servants. With growing economic pressures, a woman's financial contributions are recognized, and both individuals and governments must change their attitudes about "a woman's place."

A Lebanese family at home (above) and a Kurdish family in Iraq (right)

Societal changes, especially the gradual weakening of the traditional extended family, are also forcing changes in the way men and women relate. In the traditional Middle Eastern household, emotional openness is seen as weakness, a "womanly" quality. Yet as more couples move into apartments on their own, they must learn to relate more as equals, sharing decisions and communicating emotions.

For men brought up in the old ways, this can be a very difficult lesson. However important the changes that Middle Eastern women are seeking in their pursuit of more fulfilling lives, the changes demanded of their menfolk may be even more fundamental.

A Saudi Arabian family relaxes in their garden.

CHAPTER 7

Family and Home: Women's World

Your family, though they chew you up,
will never spit you out.

—Arabic proverb

amily is the very center of a Middle Easterner's world. More than anything else—religion, community, class—a person identifies with her or his family. People are regarded not just as individuals, but as representatives of families. Social life revolves around the family, and even in business transactions people may try to make things go smoothly by addressing each other as brother, sister, or aunt. Many people feel that if the family is undermined or significantly changed, the whole social order will be in danger.

The Tightly Knit Family

Although most nuclear families (husband, wife, and children) in urban societies live separately, they are likely to visit other family members frequently. Children grow up as part of a large group, with many cousins to play with and the security of a warm, nurturing environment. Adult children,

A family gathers for a holiday meal in Lebanon.

men as well as women, expect to live with their parents or another family member until they marry. Even in modern urban societies the idea of young people wanting to be on their own—or being "kicked out of the nest"—is almost unthinkable.

Family members support each other in many ways, emotionally as well as in practical matters. Among Lebanese Christians, for example, a funeral brings the whole family to the church, even if most never knew the deceased person. It's a way of renewing family solidarity. Families also share hardships. If one person has been insulted or mistreated, the whole family feels outraged and may think of revenge.

Family members help with expenses of education, go into business together, hire relatives, lend each other money, help each other get jobs, and fix each other's television sets. Political leaders often try to keep power within their own families and appoint family members as their associates and bodyguards.

Much of this family cohesiveness is part of the culture and a valuable source of strength for both the group and the individual. But everything has its price. Where the collective group is supreme, individuals may feel neglected or stifled. Often parents are excessively protective or controlling. Dependence on family can discourage young people from taking responsibility for themselves. Sometimes, too, people use family connections to take unfair advantage or to do dishonest things.

The Woman's Role in the Family

Muslims say that Muhammad made very clear the importance of the woman in the family. Both parents, he said, are to be equally respected. Another saying attributed to Muhammad urges: "Your mother, your mother, your mother —and then your father" (when seeking advice or support). Although the man is head of the family, it's the woman who holds the family together and transmits the group's culture and values to the next generation. Even women busily involved in careers and activities outside the home say that their family comes first, and they want their children to have a strong sense of family loyalty.

A woman must operate within the family structure; she cannot afford to ignore or alienate her family. Yet she is both supported and suppressed by the family system. She is still supposed to be subordinate to her father, brothers, husband, and sometimes even male cousins.

The Law

In the words of a young woman professor in Beirut, "If you're involved with people who don't treat you well, then the law becomes *very* important." Let us see how the law affects women's lives.

While in most Middle Eastern countries crimes and various other legal matters are covered by civil law, people's personal lives are governed by religious law. The exceptions are Tunisia, which established a progressive legal system similar to those in Western countries in 1956, and Turkey, which replaced religious law with secular law, including important rights for women, as early as 1926.

Religious law, also called Family Law or Personal Status Law, deals with all matters affecting people in their private lives: marriage, divorce, child custody, inheritance. In some important areas, such as inheritance and property ownership, Islamic law was originally meant to protect women's interests. Interpretation of the rules, however, has been debated ever since the start of Islam. Since it was men in patriarchal societies who did the debating and interpreting, Islamic law gives much greater power to the husband than to the wife and enforces the woman's inferior status.

Activists for women's rights in some countries, such as Egypt and Iraq, have been struggling for years to bring about changes in these religion-based laws. Several countries were moving in that direction for a while, but the last fifteen years or so have seen reverses. Governments in countries with strong Islamist movements feel pressure to make laws more restrictive regarding women's rights, not less.[1] It's largely because of shari'a-based family law that women in several countries—for instance Tunisia, Morocco, and Egypt—are distressed at the possibility of Islamists gaining political power.

Lebanon, with a significant Christian population, has particular problems because each of the many religious sects maintains its own laws. No one wants to talk about change, for that would mean risking the loss of some power. In 1998 a government proposal to allow civil marriage was shot down by religious leaders. Lebanon does recognize civil marriage, so long as it doesn't take place on Lebanese soil. Women activists keep attacking the injustice of this and other laws, but they find it an uphill struggle against rigid attitudes.[2]

To an observer there appear to be glaring contradictions and confusion about the woman's position in the family. Especially as she grows older, her experience and wisdom are respected. Yet the law, along with outmoded, unjust attitudes and practices, seems to work against healthy family life.

$\mathcal{A}$ Woman's $\mathcal{M}$ain Job: Children

In the traditional view, a wife's primary job is to bear and raise children, especially boys. That determines her value to a large extent, and even her identity. Islam has always encouraged large families, and traditionally many Christian families followed the same pattern.

With modern medicines and improved living standards, however, population growth in the region began to explode around the middle of the twentieth century. This is a severe problem, because most Middle Eastern countries—where much of the land is desert—do not have the natural or economic resources to provide for ever-larger populations. With the rapid growth of cities, all the social and economic ills caused by overcrowding, joblessness, and poverty intensify the problem.

Currently, population growth rates in the Middle East are among the highest in the world, with an overall average of 4 children per woman. Fertility rates range from a low of 2.5 children per woman in Tunisia to 6 for Palestinians and 7.6 for Yemenis.[3] While these figures are expected to drop, family planning is—or should be—a central issue for the majority of these countries. Egypt, for example, has a fairly serious family planning program. It's estimated that virtually all women know about some kind of birth control and close to 50 percent of married women of childbearing age use modern methods.[4] Yet the problem remains critical because

In Pakistan, women are educated in family planning at a health clinic.

Egypt's population is already too large for the land's resources and is still growing.

Among urban, educated people, a family of two or three children is typical. Rural people in some areas are also starting to limit their families but are slow to change their attitudes. For example, in southern Tunisia where family planning programs have been carried out vigorously, peasants now favor small families; but people in more tradition-bound parts of the country still feel that six children are barely enough.[5]

Sound population policies depend heavily on the role and status of women. Education, the desire to provide a better life for a smaller number of children, and jobs outside the home encourage women to limit the size of their families. But family planning remains a very complicated, sensitive matter. People's religious ideas and the attitudes of religious leaders are a major influence. Egypt's family planning program would probably not have gotten far without the approval of Muslim leaders.[6]

Political and economic problems also affect population policies. In Iran, for example, the revolutionary Islamic government first urged families to have lots of babies to strengthen the future Islamic state. Ten years later, following a devastating war with Iraq in the 1980s, the government decided it could not support a steadily increasing population. Families were then told to have no more than three children. Iraq, too, has reversed itself on this question. For a time the government promoted progressive policies, including the right of women to limit their families. Now it claims that more Iraqis are needed to develop the country and protect it from enemies. In some of the Gulf states, including Kuwait, women are encouraged to have large families to enlarge the future labor force and to reduce dependence on foreign workers.

Entrenched cultural attitudes are another potent force. In traditional Middle Eastern society a man's social image owes much to evidence of his virility: he is admired for having many children. Egyptians typically dote on children, and doubtless many parents of small families would really like more. In some cases a woman may think of children as a sort of insurance, bearing several in hopes of discouraging her husband from divorcing her or taking a second wife.

The Gulf state of Oman has an unusually high birth rate because women in certain parts of the country want very large families—twenty children, they say! The main reason is the importance of "new baby" visits. This social ritual helps determine a woman's claim to prestige and social status, which many women want to reaffirm regularly. Faced with these social attitudes, government programs are trying to persuade women at least to space births farther apart.[7]

Harem . . . or Home?

Many people in the West are fascinated by the thought of a harem—imagining it to consist of scantily clad, beautiful women lolling around inside a palace, doing nothing. European artists used to delight in portraying women of the "mysterious Orient" this way.

The harem, however, was a *place*, the part of the house where the women lived and managed the household.

A fantasy image of the Eastern harem, by Eugène Delacroix.

The word *harem* simply means "forbidden," meaning that men unrelated to the household were not allowed to enter. In some conservative Arabian and Gulf societies, there are still households where the women live apart in semi-independent, "forbidden" quarters; elsewhere the custom is outmoded.

Here, we'll have a glimpse at what home life is like for most women in the Middle East and North Africa.

The Daily Routine

A middle-class homemaker in cities and towns has many of the modern appliances found in American homes: refrigerator, washing machine, perhaps a microwave and dishwasher. The homemaker's day, however, is more occupied with housework than that of most American women. She may go out every morning to the vegetable shop, the butcher shop, and the bakery, daily fresh bread is essential. In some large cities she may choose between well-stocked supermarkets and convenient little neighborhood groceries.

In Saudi Arabia and the Gulf states the supermarkets are huge and ultramodern. Because Saudi Arabian women are not allowed to drive, often their husbands do the grocery shopping. Many women do go alone however, their drivers waiting outside.

Middle Eastern cooking is delicious, but it takes a lot of time to mince the vegetables, stuff the vine leaves, deep-fry the meat-filled pastries, and so forth. A homemaker usually devotes most of her morning to preparing the midday meal, traditionally the main meal of the day. When company is expected, the food may take days to prepare.

In rural areas, women live much as their grandmothers did. Some bake bread outdoors in a very ancient type of earthen oven, still in use from North Africa to Iran. Or they may take their dough to the village communal oven, the main place where women can meet for a chat in the course of their day's work. A rural woman's routine, as in Yemen, is also likely to include a lot of walking: a hike to an outdoor market, a search for wood for fuel, and a trip to the river or public faucet for water, which she carries home in a container balanced on her head. When her daughters are old enough, they usually fetch the water. In Lebanon and Syria, the village "fountain" used to be the social gathering spot—where girls hoped to be noticed by the young men.

Today's peasant woman may live in a hut with an earth floor and sleep on padding that is folded up and pushed to one side every morning. But she very likely owns one household item that her grandmother would not have dreamed of: a television set. Most rural homes in the Tunisian and Jordanian countryside, for example, boast a television and possibly a satellite dish.

Wherever people have leisure and TV, they watch almost constantly. Television has had a profound impact on women, especially in rural environments, making them more aware of the need for change. But television can also undermine valuable aspects of traditional cultures. When young Bedouin women in the desert see Egyptian movies on television, they want the material things of modern life and lose interest in their own crafts and clothing.[8]

Kitchen and Culture

In the Middle East, kitchens are not like the large, comfortable, multipurpose rooms of typical American homes. In traditional houses and older city apartments, they are usually small and dark, as if the place where a woman does most of her work does not need to be pleasant. The author (EM) once visited a Moroccan family in the quaint old part of the city known as the Casbah. The wife and her daughters brought out plate after plate of Arab sweets. Later I asked to see the kitchen and was shown a dark corner with a single small kerosene burner for cooking. Had they prepared all the refreshments *there*? Matter-of-factly they nodded yes. This happened in the 1970s; today the woman's daughters and granddaughters undoubtedly expect better.

Kitchens in modern buildings are more roomy and well designed. But as a rule, the kitchen in a Middle Eastern home remains a workplace. Social life goes on in a sitting room, stuffed full of as much furniture and decorative objects as the family can afford.

While urban apartments have modern bathrooms, the public baths—an important feature of Middle Eastern cities of the past—still exist. The bath may consist of a pool of warm water, possibly showers, or individual marble sinks where a person sloshes herself with warm water. For many a woman of the poorer classes, the public bath is the only place where she can get clean. Just as important, there she can relax, gossip, and perhaps, as in Egypt, consult the local authority on magic spells. The steamy shadows of a bathhouse make a good place for practitioners of magic to carry on their business.

A modern kitchen makes life easier for this Lebanese woman (top). In a Jordanian village a woman bakes bread in the traditional way (bottom).

Housework

Who helps with the housework? Daughters, of course. If a woman has no help from family, she'll hire a servant if possible. In Egypt, where many poor people need jobs, most middle-class women have at least a part-time maid to shop, clean, and cook. In other countries, however, the indigenous supply of maids has vanished. As girls from lower-class families have gotten some schooling, they have found better jobs. Today, both in Lebanon and in the Gulf countries, almost all domestic workers come from Sri Lanka, Ethiopia, or the Philippines.

How do women who work outside the home manage their housework? Will the husband help? The author (EM) put this question to a Tunisian woman, a former government minister of social affairs. "Definitely," she answered. "These days, in young families, the husband and wife must share

This Afghan woman carries dishes at her home in Kandahar.

housework. They can't manage any other way." But another professional woman in Tunis answered with a resounding *no*. "Tunisian women work hard," she said; "they're employed full-time and responsible for the home." In any case, when guests are present, the wife does all the work.

The double work burden weighs women down in other countries as well. In Syria, women complain of having to be "super professional, super wife, and super mother."[9] Yet it's still hard for many women to see a man washing dishes or doing other "menial" jobs around the house; it flies in the face of complex, deep-seated attitudes. Some women would be outraged if their husbands attempted to help in the kitchen. That would be a reflection on the wife's competence, an infringement on her domain, and another way for the man to assert his authority over her. No easy answers. But some change in the traditional division of domestic labor seems inevitable.

When Work Is Done

Whatever other cultural or charitable activities a woman may have, there is one leisure activity she almost certainly pursues: visiting.

Lebanese women visit and chat over a cup of tea.

In the Levant countries, morning visits with relatives and neighbors to drink coffee are called *subhiyya*, from the Arabic word for morning, *sabah*. Afternoon visits are more elaborate. In summer the hostess will offer a cool drink, then pass around a plate of chocolates—once. The poorest woman is quick to offer a casual visitor whatever she has, even if just a few peanuts.

Most important is the coffee or, more commonly in North Africa, glasses of tea. Coffee, tiny cups of strong black brew, is basic to Middle Eastern society. At a fairly formal visit in Jordan, coffee is always the last thing served, and the timing can be tricky. If the hostess serves it too soon, it looks as though she wants her visitors to leave; but if she delays too long, the guests may wonder how long they'll have to stay.

In Yemen, women visit almost every afternoon. These gatherings are important, reflecting a woman's status and wealth. The custom of chewing *qat*, a leaf with a mildly narcotic effect, is almost universal among men and now increasingly popular with women. The amount of qat a husband gives his wife becomes a way of showing status, as it is rather expensive. Although Yemenis value qat-chewing as part of their cultural identity, it does lead to some health and social problems.[10]

Throughout the region, visits are expected on religious holidays and family events such as weddings, births, deaths, and the arrival of a family member from abroad. People also drop in without invitation or announcement. This old custom is becoming more difficult to deal with these days, when so many women are employed outside the home. Nevertheless, casual visiting is a characteristic of social life that Middle Easterners miss when they go to live in other countries.

Visits are not simply "women's business." In modern societies of the Levant and North Africa, families make social calls together, men and women mingling just as in

American homes. The children are expected to behave properly. Most young people learn to be poised and well mannered in adult company, considering themselves part of the family group.

At the other extreme are the gender-segregated societies of Saudi Arabia and some of the Gulf states. There, women's visiting takes on awesome dimensions. At least once a year a middle-class Saudi Arabian woman may entertain fifty to a hundred women in her home, with live music (all-female bands), lavish food, and everyone in stylish clothes, including the last word in designer jeans.[11]

For most women in Middle Eastern societies, life could hardly go on without visiting because of the emotional support it provides. This is especially true in villages where there is no other form of recreation. Visiting is also highly important in societies where husbands and wives have little to do with each other or when a woman is trapped in an unhappy family situation. Together, women may be able to stir up family or neighborhood opinion and shame a wayward son or bad-tempered husband into better behavior. Visiting can help hold a community together, as women keep abreast of what is going on and then inform their husbands.

Whether a party on the Saudi Arabian scale or a brief chat between neighbors, visiting is an essential part of women's personal lives. It can have a marked effect not only on their emotional condition but on the health of their families and communities.

8

Veiling

A girl possesses nothing but a veil and a tomb.
—Saudi Arabian proverb

The thicker the veil, the less worth lifting.
—Tunisian proverb.

*I*n the last thirty or forty years, numerous Middle Eastern women have made the momentous step from private to public life: education, paid employment, cultural activities, politics, sports. Yet along with this liberation has come renewed focus on the veil, that persistent symbol in many people's eyes of oppression.

The practice of veiling, and all that it implies about concealment of women, may be the most difficult aspect of Middle Eastern lifeways for people in the West to understand. It lends itself to wildly inaccurate stereotypes, such as the notion that all women must spend their lives shrouded in long black robes. Yet the fact that people in the West misunderstand the veil is hardly surprising, for it is a controversial subject among people in the Arab and Muslim worlds as well. It means different things to different people and can be interpreted in a number of ways. In the words of an Egyptian writer, "Emancipation can be expressed by wearing the veil or by removing it. It can be secular or religious. It can represent tradition or resistance."[1]

A Short History of the Veil

Both in the West and in much of the Middle East, *veiling* is the popular word for a woman concealing her hair and body, and sometimes her face, for religious reasons. A more accurate term, however, is *hijab*, which means simply "cover." Although in the past Christian and Jewish women also covered in public, the custom is now primarily Islamic. What does the holy book of Islam have to say about it?

The Qur'an calls upon all believers, men and women, to behave and dress in a modest fashion. The most specific instruction the Qur'an gives to women is as follows: they should lower their gaze, draw their veils over their bosoms, and reveal their adornments only to the men and other women in their own households.[2] Just what "adornments" means is not clear. It could mean jewelry or hair or the natural beauty of a woman's face and figure. Nowhere does the Qur'an explicitly require Muslim women to veil heavily or cover their faces. Thus the custom of concealing women appears not to have been an essential part of Islam at the start.

As the Arab Muslims spread throughout the Middle East in the seventh century C.E., they came in contact with other peoples of the region who did seclude their women. Among the Persians and Byzantine Christians, wealthy women wore veils and stayed inside their homes as a mark of social status. Soon upper-class Muslims adopted these customs. Seclusion became an important part of the patriarchal code of honor and of Islam—not necessarily Islam as it was taught by Muhammad but as it came to be practiced.

The veil has always been a middle- and upper-class custom. Peasant women and lower-class urban women usually did not cover because they had to work in the fields and the streets, where such garments would be a hindrance.

Covering Takes Many Forms

Many types of head covering are simply part of traditional dress. Egyptian peasant women wear colorful kerchiefs on their heads and full-length black cloaks over their flowered dresses. In Tunisia, the traditional garment is a long white cloth called a *sefsari*, wrapped gracefully over the head and around the body. Perhaps some head-to-foot coverings originated in ideas of modesty, but they are really traditional dress rather than a way of concealing women from the world.

Until the last few decades, some middle-class women in Egyptian cities wore a short, thin black veil with gold trim over the lower part of the face. A Bedouin woman in the Sinai Peninsula today covers her nose and mouth with a small piece of bright red silk richly decorated with old coins and beads, almost like face jewelry. Moroccan women in traditional dress conceal all but their eyes with a skillfully draped combination of headdress and face covering, usually made of a plain, pastel-colored fabric.

Two forms of traditional veiling on Afghan women

In Beirut, conservative Muslim women used to wear a black cloth over the hair and a second short black cloth over the entire face. Among the Druze people of Lebanon, a young girl wears a thin white cloth loosely over her head until the age of fifteen. After that age, a devout woman wears the white cloth in such a way as to cover her hair and her mouth and chin. Women in parts of rural Yemen cover themselves completely with heavy black cloth, all but a slit for their eyes; they even work in the fields that way.[3]

All women in Saudi Arabia are required by the government to cover themselves top to toe with a black cloak called an *abbayah*; in the most conservative cities, the cloak must cover their faces completely. In very conservative communities of the Gulf states, some women still wear a heavy leather mask over their faces. Although women from these countries generally are glad to shed the hijab as soon as they go abroad, sometimes a woman can be seen visiting in Cairo, for instance, completely covered by thick black fabric— while her husband wears a short-sleeved shirt.

This is just a sample of different forms of traditional veiling worn in recent decades and even today, underscoring the wide variety of lifeways and styles among Middle Eastern women.

Veiling in the Twentieth Century

Early in the twentieth century a few upper-class women in Egypt began to speak out against practices that kept women subservient. Starting in the 1920s, more and more women discarded the face veil, until by the 1960s few Egyptian women wore the hijab at all. Women in other societies adopting modern ways were likewise putting away their veils.

The 1970s, however, brought a surprising change. In cities where most women had repudiated the custom, some were starting to wear the veil again. Once again, Egypt led the way, this time in this revival of the hijab, which was quickly followed in other countries. The new forms of veiling, generally termed "Islamic dress," are different from the traditional, but again there is plenty of variety. Iranian women wear a head-to-foot black cloak called a *chador*, a traditional garment. Early in the revolutionary Islamic regime that took over Iran in 1979, the government required all women to wear this garment; now it is more lenient and permits colored head scarves and long coats. In Jordan, a conservative university student may cover her hair carefully—not a wisp showing—with a plain scarf of white or black and wear a long, sober-colored coat. In Tunisia, too, although the government has discouraged the practice of veiling, some city women dress in this way.

A visual contrast is the hijab chosen by some Muslim women, especially young ones, in the almost-anything-goes city of Beirut. Styles change from year to year. For a while some girls wore head scarves and long dresses in brilliant colors, decidedly "Look at me!" outfits. A head scarf with baggy sweater and tight jeans is a continuing style. In 2002 some young Beiruti women wore a narrow, form-fitting skirt to the ankles. Of course many others wore a much more subdued hijab, consisting of a head scarf and long coat.

The same is true in Egyptian cities: variety and changing styles. High-style Islamic costume was seen in the early 1990s, with headdresses of soft fabrics trimmed with tassels and pearls. The majority of women who choose to veil today wear a simple head scarf, either plain or in a colorful print, along with a full-length skirt or regular Western-style clothes. Once the author (EM) spent some time in a government office talking with a woman who wore the hijab in a stylish but not showy fashion. When asked my opinion of the Islamic costume, I said it could be quite attractive. "Yes," the woman answered, pleased. "That's what we want. Modesty—with elegance."

Yemeni women appear at the United Nations Fourth World Conference in a strict form of veiling.

At the other extreme are the few urban Egyptian women who adopt a total hijab. In addition to a plain capelike head-dress and a long unadorned gown, they wear heavy gloves; they conceal their faces behind two pieces of cloth that leave only a tiny slit for the eyes. The decision as to what sort of hijab she will wear, therefore, is a personal one among many Muslim women. And not all women, by any means, wear the hijab. The percentage of women who cover differs from country to country and from community to community.

Revival of Veiling

Now for the vital question: Why are so many women, including young educated women, choosing to revive a practice that seemed outmoded only twenty or thirty years ago?

Revival of the hijab is at the core of assertive Islamic consciousness, which appeared in the 1970s in Egypt. Today Islamism attracts many people who find it a source of strength in their own lives and believe it points the way to a healthy society. Islamists underscore the importance of woman's traditional role as wife, mother, and center of family. Along with this emphasis—which does not necessarily mean seclusion in the home or denial of public activity—goes the view that women should dress modestly and adopt the hijab.

Some reasons are more personal. Many a Middle Eastern woman today finds herself in a world dramatically unlike that of her mother and grandmother, and may feel threatened by the social changes. Her religion, with the veil as constant reminder, can give her reassurance. For many women, hijab can be understood as an overall attitude, symbolizing values such as honor, decency, and appropriate behavior.

A woman may wish to assert her religious status visually. Her hijab expresses her identity as a Muslim, as if she is announcing publicly, "I am a Muslim and take pride in my religion and culture." By communicating this message, the veil serves a practical purpose as well. When a woman in a conservative neighborhood goes out to work dressed in hijab, it tells her neighbors that she is a virtuous, proper Muslim woman: no one should think ill of her because she works outside her home.[4] In the workplace or the university classroom, a veiled woman feels safe in the company of the men she works with or the strangers she may meet. They will regard her only as a coworker or fellow student, not as a "sex object." At the same time, the hijab is an unambiguous sign of femininity, which can lessen men's fears of a woman encroaching into the male sphere. In hijab, a woman tells the world, "I am a good woman, a pious Muslim, and a threat to no one. Don't hassle me."

Another advantage of the veil, some women argue, is that it allows a woman to stop thinking about her looks and to concentrate on more important things, such as her job, studies, and family. Those who support this argument point to Western women—whom they know about mostly from television, movies, and the sensational press—as an example they do not want to follow.

Young Women Who Veil

The Islamist movement started largely with idealistic—and in a way rebellious—university students in Egypt. These young people were not turning their backs on or retreating from the world; they wanted to make their religious beliefs very much a part of the world. The veil confirmed the women's cultural identity and faith in the relevance of Islamic ideals, while asserting independence from Western culture. Through Islam, they opposed both the legacy of Western colonialism and what they saw as the materialistic, power-hungry drive of Western nations to dominate. The veil became a symbol of their resistance to what they found wrong in the world.[5]

For many young women the veil was a way of telling their parents, "You of the older generation put your faith in a secular, modern system. But look! Today we have more problems than ever. Only through Islam can we hope to solve them."[6]

There are, however, some reasons besides deeply held conviction why girls may cover. Some find that the veil not only does protect and free them in the high school or university, but that when they wear the head covering and modest dress, their families feel reassured and are inclined not to keep such a tight rein on them. This makes it easier to go out and spend time with friends, including young men.

Many levels of piety and principle, it appears, are involved in decisions to veil.

Thoughtful women point out that the hijab is no substitute for a genuinely virtuous life. Najat, a young professional woman in Cairo, commented: "My brothers now think they should marry only a woman who veils, but I tell them that wearing the hijab is no guarantee of a woman's honesty or kindness. Muslims should focus on the most important values of Islam, not just the outward expression, the hijab." Najat, incidentally, does veil, for modesty. As a woman who has chosen the exceptional path of living alone in the city, she has doubtless made a sensible decision.[7]

Still, Questions . . .

Personal faith, cultural confidence, reassurance, fashion: all these motives help explain choices regarding the veil. But some women undoubtedly do not make a free choice. Family pressures, especially from husbands, fathers, and even sons, are powerful in women's lives. Sometimes employers require that a woman wear the veil. In places, it's probably a question of patriarchal control. In the bazaars of some Syrian cities, for example, a head scarf allows a woman to move about freely, whereas an unveiled woman might receive muttered insults.[8]

Another form of coercion comes from Islamist movements. Women in these groups are expected to wear the veil both to indicate religious conviction and to demonstrate political solidarity. At the University of Aden in the southern part of Yemen, which had a politically progressive government in the 1970s and 1980s, few women veiled in recent years. Today, however, virtually all female students and professors wear the hijab. Islamist pressure on their families, some say, forces them to do so.[9] Islamic dress, including total covering, is now seen commonly on the streets of Kuwait—a very recent development.

What changes in veiling the next few years will bring is impossible to predict. Because to some extent Islamism is a reaction against Western influence, political developments on the international level may affect how a woman covers her hair in Tehran or Casablanca.

A critical question remains. Islam calls for both men and women to dress modestly—yet today all the emphasis is on *women* covering themselves. Why should a woman have to cloak herself in a visual announcement that she is a good woman in order to walk down the street without being harassed? One basic explanation is not as widely discussed as the arguments in favor of veiling that we have just seen, but neither is it a secret.

A popular Islamic leader and television personality in Cairo explained it in this way: The sight of a woman's beauty—especially her hair—is so tantalizing that it can be intolerably distracting to men. It turns their thoughts away from pious, proper behavior.[10] An adolescent youth suffers from frustrated sexual desire, and a middle-aged man thinks of discarding his wife for a younger woman.

Thus to prevent men from experiencing this emotional agitation, it is the duty of all women, regardless of age or condition, to conceal their hair and the shape of their bodies. Women must behave in such a way as to remove temptation from men's paths—including strangers on the street. Women are held responsible for men's emotions and conduct.

To sum up: A woman's assertion of her religious and cultural identity may inspire her to put on the veil. Her freedom to leave her home and do what she needs or wants to do may depend on her wearing the veil. The social setting in which she lives may require the veil. But the ultimate meaning of covering still raises some disturbing questions.

9

Women's Health

*My health is more precious than my wealth,
my anklets, and earrings.*

—Tunisian proverb

*I*n the Middle Ages medical knowledge among the Arabs far surpassed the Europeans' crude notions. Some of the medieval Arab practices were handed down through the centuries as what we call folk medicine. Women were masters of this art, sometimes with an almost uncanny skill in healing.

Modern Medicine

The importance of women's health is gaining attention as a social concern. A 1996 survey of women's views in Jordan found general agreement that women should be kept healthy and brought up in a healthy lifestyle. Like education, however, the emphasis was on the social importance: a woman's ability to meet her family's needs by keeping well. While providing a useful teaching tool, the study said little about awareness of a woman's right to good health for her own sake.[1]

With the rapid urbanization of the Middle East, modern medical treatment is within reach of the large majority of people. Most hospitals in the cities of Lebanon, Jordan, Saudi Arabia, and the Gulf states, for instance, are excellent and can be reached by car within a few hours.

In remote rural areas, not surprisingly, it's a different story. Medical facilities are rare and usually poorly equipped; a woman experiencing severe problems in childbirth, for example, has little chance of surviving. In Yemen, the government spends less on health than any other Middle Eastern country, and the childbirth mortality rate is one of the highest in the world. Health centers in rural areas are primitive, often lacking electricity and running water. When women can get to a hospital, they find that most of the medical personnel are men, which offends their ideas of modesty.[2]

Afghan women in a run-down hospital in Kabul

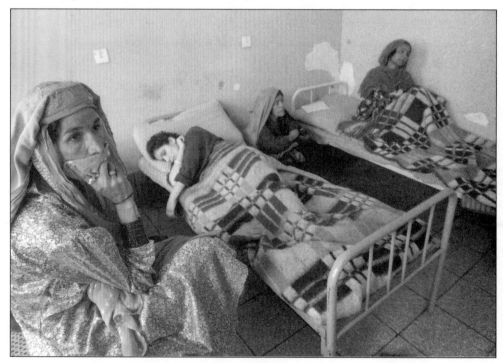

Iraq offers a uniquely tragic example of how forces entirely beyond people's control can devastate public health. Formerly Iraq was a prosperous nation with good medical facilities and highly trained personnel. Because of the trade sanctions that the United Nations, under pressure from the United States, imposed on Iraq following the 1991 Gulf war, medical materials have been reduced to a tiny fraction of what is needed. Mothers must watch their sick children die from lack of the most basic medical treatment. For years child mortality rates in Iraq have been appalling.

Modern Plagues

Regions adjacent to the Middle East—Africa and Eastern Europe—are afflicted with high rates of the most frightening of modern plagues: AIDS. In the Arab/Muslim countries, rates of AIDS infection appear to be so low that they are not reported in international surveys[3]—or else there is not yet willingness to recognize the urgency of this matter. There are, however, increasing numbers of cases, with women among the victims. When this happens, especially in Lebanon, the woman is hit a double blow: she knows she got the infection from her husband, who got it from some other sexual partner, probably on a business trip to Africa.[4]

A few efforts are under way to publicize the problem of sexually transmitted diseases. Tunisia has a national campaign that targets women in particular, underlining a woman's right to "say no." In Lebanon, the National AIDS Program focuses more on men, emphasizing monogamous behavior and traditional values. Plans also include introducing education about AIDS in secondary schools. A progressive women's magazine in Iran, *Zanan*, has dealt with the problem. As yet, however, AIDS awareness is high priority in the Middle East.

An Ancient Scourge, Still Prevalent

A subject that has attracted much attention in recent years is the practice of female genital mutilation (FGM), also sometimes called female circumcision. This is actually a social problem, tied up with questions of male control over women, obsession with family honor, and the grip of unquestioned tradition. But because this practice also has such dire effects on the psychological and physical health of girls and women, we'll discuss it largely from the health perspective.

Tradition imposes a cruel fate on many girls in Egypt.

FGM means cutting away part or even all of a young girl's external genital organs. Found mostly among some African peoples, the custom is also prevalent in Egypt. It is almost unknown elsewhere in the Middle East.

Although some Muslim women think the practice is required by religion, Islam does not require or condone FGM in any way. In 1995 the Grand Mufti, the highest cleric in Egypt, gave his official view that there is nothing in the Qur'an to support it.[5] Furthermore, FGM is done not only by Muslims in Egypt but by many Coptic Christians, which shows that it is a regional practice, not a religious one.

Until the 1990s, very little was known about the extent of the custom in Egypt; the subject was almost never discussed openly. Now it is a hot topic among progressive women's groups. According to recent estimates, around 95 percent of women in Egypt—urban and rural, educated and uneducated—are victims of FGM.[6]

Those who believe in FGM claim that it is necessary to control a girl's strong sexual impulses. It will ensure that she remains a virgin until marriage and then stays faithful to her husband. As a so-called female rite of passage, it "makes a girl a woman," "purifies" her, makes her more "smooth and beautiful." Despite the pain and other health problems it causes, the practice is perpetuated by the very women who have suffered it. They believe unquestioningly that it is essential for both femininity and chastity. As an Egyptian peasant woman put it, "Circumcision is absolutely necessary. I don't know why, but it is a tradition."[7]

Where the custom is followed, men will not marry a girl who has not been circumcised. Thus it is another form of male control over the female. For a mother to go against custom and *not* have her daughter circumcised would doom the girl to life without marriage in a society where every woman expects marriage.[8]

Very often, FGM is performed under unhygienic conditions. In addition to the fright and pain a young girl suffers, she may get severe, sometimes fatal, infections and hemorrhages. As an adult, she will most likely experience difficult childbirth, little sexual pleasure, and chronic infections. In her story "Bahiyya's Eyes," the Egyptian writer Alifa Rifaat tells about an old Egyptian peasant woman thinking back over her sad life and the effect of "what those women did to me with the razor."[9]

Most educated Egyptian women, and women in other Arab countries, firmly condemn FGM. Since the 1970s women's organizations have been trying to publicize the problem. The Cairo Family Planning Association, founded by the pioneering activist for women's causes Aziza Hussein, has been a leader in this effort to educate women. A group working with the "trashpickers community" in Cairo requires attendance at classes in hygiene and health and provides training for income-producing skills. Through education they have succeeded in persuading many of these young women to stop FGM in their own families.[10]

Governmental and medical groups have attempted to discourage the practice for the past twenty-five years or so, with little success. In 1979, FGM was banned in Egypt, but the law had no effect. In 1994 a circumcision was actually shown on television in Cairo, which unfortunately produced a backlash defending the practice. For a while FGM operations were allowed in public hospitals, in the hope of discouraging secret operations in unhygienic conditions. In 1996 the Ministry of Health prohibited the practice, but soon afterward, under public pressure, had to allow it again.

Organizations and publications continue their efforts to educate the public. But because the notion that this operation is necessary is so fixed in many people's minds, the campaign is inevitably a slow, tough process. For example, recently the author (EM) taught English to a group of Somali and Eritrean young men in Cairo. One wrote a paper describing his country's customs, which included female genital mutilation. He explained matter-of-factly that it was necessary to prevent girls from getting "wild." Then, in all innocence, he asked whether we did it in my country. I was uncertain how to react: a good lecture to set him straight? Then I decided differently, and I can only hope it was the right decision. "No," I said briefly, as though dismissing the idea as unthinkable in a modern society.

10

Women at Work

A woman with no purse is a shameful thing.

—Arab proverb

$\mathscr{A}$t a Tunis hotel one morning in 1995, the author (EM) spoke with a professor from the University of Tunis, a young woman who had already published several books and worked as an equal partner with her husband, also a scholar. Later that day, while walking in a park just across the street from the hotel, I noticed another couple, elderly. The old woman trudged painfully up the hill, bent double under a great bundle of sticks. Her husband walked upright, carrying not so much as a twig.

Even in rapidly modernizing countries such as Tunisia, there are extremes in "woman's work."

Why Middle Eastern Women Work

Today it's a fact of life for the majority of women in the Middle East that they will do some kind of nonhomemaking work. But if home life in the Middle East is so important, why do women want to work outside the home?

Women sort wool in Syria.

The main reason is the same as for women anywhere: most need money. Increasing numbers of women have no men to support them, whether due to war, imprisonment, sickness, unemployment, divorce, or other causes. These women must work to support themselves and their children. But even with employed husbands, many women need to work in these years of steadily rising prices. Although there are some amazingly wealthy people in the region, the great majority of families have to struggle to make ends meet. A two-income family is becoming the norm.

The real news, however, is that so many Middle Eastern women desire—even demand—to work outside the home, and for reasons other than financial. They see their work as an expression of individual ability, independence, self-esteem, and growth. Among many Tunisian women, for example, work is almost glorified. Their mothers and grandmothers led illiterate, cloistered lives at home, but when Tunisia gained independence from France in 1956, one of the new nation's first acts was to adopt a constitution guaranteeing women many basic rights. Anyone who has seen women police officers briskly directing traffic in downtown Tunis or in Istanbul, Turkey, knows that these women are very much part of the male work world.

Here are some other examples from a recent survey of Tunisian women. A lawyer, age twenty-six: "If my future husband should tell me to stop working, I would not do so—because work is part of me; it's like the air I breathe. It's hope." A journalist, age thirty-six: "The work of women is also an enrichment for society. Women have a different manner from men in approaching problems; they are more sensitive." A bank employee, age thirty-two: "My work allows me to assert myself in my family and in society. If I had not gone to work, I wouldn't have won my liberty."[1] Another example comes from Lebanon, where a businessman told the author (EM) about a young woman on his staff, married and a new mother. "She leaves the baby with a maid, who costs most of her salary . . . but she would never accept not to work."

Of course, not all are this enthusiastic. The typical working woman has to carry two jobs: her outside work and her almost single-handed care of home and family.

What They Do

"The first woman to do such-and-such" was a familiar phrase in the Middle East during the 1970s and 1980s: "the first Jordanian woman pilot," "the first Kuwaiti woman publisher," "the first woman broadcaster in Qatar." In Egypt, Lebanon, Tunisia, and Turkey, a few women have been active in the professions at least since the 1940s. Today women are well represented in medicine, dentistry, law, and banking, along with the professions that have been more hospitable to women, such as journalism and library science. Tunisian women account for one-third of the physicians in the country, more than half of the dentists, and two-thirds of the pharmacists.[2] In Turkey, about one out of eight engineers is a woman.

Women have been employed in office work in some countries for decades. Women are also increasingly successful at running things at the high managerial level: schools, university departments, hospitals, institutes, government departments, television stations, construction companies. In 1994, a large European airline appointed a Tunisian, for the first time as

A travel agent in Damascus

regional director for North Africa: a woman employed by the airline for twenty-two years. An American researcher visiting the Ministry of Labor in Turkey noted a marked contrast between the "plodding bureaucratic style" of the men and the "cooperative and efficient manner" of their female supervisor.[3]

Numerous women entrepreneurs have started their own businesses. Most of these are small, in textiles and fashion, but a few Tunisian women are doing multi-million-dollar business in such varied fields as security services, shipping, and pharmaceutical products. Other women run their own bakeries, bookshops, publicity and consulting firms, art galleries, and so on. A plastic container company in Oman is the single-handed creation of a young woman who worked for ten years to save up capital and in less than two years was doing a booming business.[4]

A flower vendor in Beirut

In many countries, tourism is a good field for women's employment. Likewise, in this site of ancient civilizations, archaeology attracts some women. Most women in white-collar jobs, however, are still employed as school teachers and office workers. The great majority of elementary school teachers in virtually all countries are women. At higher levels of education, male teachers still dominate, although there are many female university professors.

Nursing: one of the typical "women's professions"? Not in the Middle East. Nursing has long been considered a low-status occupation because a nurse may have to do dirty work and treat male patients. Lebanon was a pioneer in training nurses, starting in 1908 at the American University of Beirut; but even in that country, many people still have a negative impression of nursing. Although the governments of the Gulf states have given nurses' training high priority, they still depend heavily on nurses from East Asian countries.

Factory jobs are the answer for many working-class women. The idea was resisted at first in the more conservative countries. When a Chinese-run textile factory opened in Yemen in the late 1970s, government officials said women would not work there because of cultural restraints; but an announcement on the radio produced 600 applicants.[5] Now Morocco and Tunisia lead in factory employment of women, followed by Egypt, Lebanon, and Syria, mainly in textiles, clothing, food-processing, and chemical industries. Although typically paid less than their male counterparts, many women find satisfaction in their work life and value the mutual support they find on the job.[6]

In some countries that have trade unions, such as Morocco, Tunisia, and Lebanon, a few strong women are edging their way into active roles in their unions. A young Tunisian woman described problems of intimidation by bosses and apathy among other female workers. "In spite of everything," she said, "I intend to continue my union activity—it's a duty, I feel."[7] In Morocco in 1995, some 500 women textile workers went on strike to protest unfair treatment and the rape of their union's general secretary—an indication of not only the threat of violence toward assertive female workers but also women's ability to mobilize.[8]

Various organizations assist poor women to earn an income and achieve some independence through self-help projects. Since the late 1980s a Cairo group has been helping *zebbaleen* (trash collectors) women learn crafts such as rug weaving and papermaking. From the sales of these products the women earn an income while acquiring some education and a sense of self-esteem. Another organization in Cairo sells handcrafts made by village women—including burn victims, who are often ostracized because of disfigurement.

A survey of women's work in the Middle East must include one of the most surprising of all female occupations: military bodyguard. Shortly after he took power in Libya in the 1970s, Colonel Muammar al-Qaddafi has called for military training of women, a radical move in Libyan society. His formidable force of young female bodyguards profess great loyalty to their leader.[9]

Social Attitudes: Help and Hindrance

Thus far, the picture of women at work in the Middle East looks promising. But social attitudes and expectations are still strong forces.

Until recently women in Algeria, for instance, had to contend with the persistent idea that a working woman must have questionable morals.[10] In parts of Iran, for a woman to work publicly implied that her husband was unable to support her—or control her. While such objections are no longer a significant problem in most places, Middle Eastern women still feel the constraint of family obligations more than do most Americans and Europeans.

Talented Lebanese artists, for example, agree that it's almost impossible for a married woman to devote herself to art professionally.[11]

On one hand, families can be an asset. A financially well-off family, modern in outlook, is likely to encourage its daughters to seek the kind of work those young women wish. Families may have connections (called *wasta*) that can make a girl's job hunt easier, although some young women rebel against this and wish to be hired only on their own merits.[12] Families can also help by looking after the children. For many women, the support of the extended family in this way is absolutely essential. Day-care centers and preschools do exist in the cities of some countries—Syria, Tunisia, Lebanon, and Egypt, for example—but the quality of such care varies. Good preschools can take a large bite out of a woman's pay.

On the other hand, sometimes families seriously hinder or prevent a young woman from pursuing her goals. This was the case with an Algerian university professor named Louisa, who grew up in a mountain village. Louisa's father could see the value of a woman being able to support herself; his younger brothers, however, were outraged when he let his daughter go to school, saying it would shame the family. "The irony," Louisa adds, "is that now, twenty years later, my uncles permit their daughters to do what they wouldn't allow for me. I'm happy for those girls, of course, . . . but how much hardship could have been avoided!"[13]

Some husbands feel threatened when their wives take a job outside the home, but others are proud. At a leadership training workshop in Cairo, an unusually assertive young woman, in hijab, gave her husband credit for encouraging her to go to college and pursue a career. "I was ready to settle for staying home with babies and the whole domestic thing," she said, "but he wouldn't let me!"[14]

Militantly conservative Islamists would explicitly deny women the right to work. Less rigid Islamists—including many women—insist that women should be able to have jobs and careers. This right, they claim, does not detract from a strong and virtuous society based on Islamic principles.[15]

What Governments Do for Women at Work

In most countries of the Middle East and North Africa, government policies uphold the rights of married women and mothers to be employed. Typically, women are promised paid maternity leave of six to ten weeks—one year in Iraq. Labor codes in several countries, especially Egypt and Syria, are generally quite fair. Nonetheless, employers can sometimes find ways to get around them. For instance, Egyptian companies that employ more than 100 women are supposed to provide child-care facilities; but many, to avoid this requirement, are careful to keep the number of women employees just below that level.[16]

For Egyptian women, government policies have resulted in some other benefits and problems. In 1952 a revolutionary socialist regime started drastic economic and social reforms, including "jobs for everyone." Government offices and government-run businesses had to hire more people than were really needed. In the 1990s the move was back to private enterprise, and as companies tried to trim their payrolls women employees were likely to be let go first.

Jordan adopted policies to encourage employment of women because of practical needs. In the 1960s and 1970s many of Jordan's professional and skilled workers sought employment in the oil-rich Gulf states. To make up for the male "brain drain," the Jordanian government stepped up education of girls and training opportunities for women. Unfortunately, when employment opportunities in the Gulf states shrank, the men came home and the women's job outlook got tighter.

In some cases government leaders have reversed their ideologies concerning women in the work world. The Islamic government of Iran at first told women to go back to the kitchen, but later encouraged them to go out to work. Now Iranian women play an important role in the workforce at all levels, as professionals, intellectuals, and factory workers.[17]

Saudi Arabian women present a special case. Their right to work is controlled by a powerful combination of conservative Islamic ideology and government policies, which works both for and against women's interests. Because of strict segregation of the sexes, two separate work worlds have developed. Just as women have their own schools, they have separate professions and businesses: medical clinics, banks, stores, newspapers—all for women only, all owned and run by women. Some women's businesses have grown tremendously in recent years, thanks in part to the Internet.[18] Thus Saudi women do not have to compete with men in developing their abilities and pursuing their careers. Yet they are allowed to deal with only half of humankind and could not change matters if they wished to.

The role of government can have a profound effect, not just on working conditions and rights but also on broad social trends. Because government typically offers educated women the best opportunities for jobs, whether as office workers or teachers, women are increasingly dependent on the state for their well-being—and less dependent on the male head of the family. The consequences for many areas of Middle Eastern life, from family authority to women's participation in politics, will doubtless be far-reaching.

Rural Women at Work

Until recently, when researchers gathered statistics on women workers in developing countries, the Middle Eastern countries produced very low figures: at most, women accounted for 20 percent of the total labor force. But women who did agricultural work were being overlooked. If women in agriculture were counted, they would make up a large percentage of the national and regional labor force.

Women in agricultural communities—at least half of all women in Egypt, Yemen, Jordan, and the North African nations—have no choice but to work. They cook, bake bread, tend gardens and field crops and livestock, take care of the family's clothes—all the age-old tasks of rural women. Often they are still working long after their men, finished for the day, have settled down at the local café.

These women are probably the most in need of change in their working conditions. Small projects designed to increase women's money-earning ability and empowerment can help, but more basic is finding new ways for women to participate in agricultural production and get a fairer share of the profits. Fortunately, governments and international organizations are now more aware of the importance of rural women when they plan development projects.[19]

As agricultural technology becomes more modernized, women's roles change. Traditionally women's work gave them a certain power. Now some of those jobs, such as weeding and harvesting, are being taken over by machines, and it's men who run machines. As a result, women may become less important in the family and community. Or the opposite can happen. In farm families in central Turkey, women now have more time for their own enterprises: making yogurt and butter, knitting woolen socks. The sale of such products brings them income and new power in their society.

Sometimes, when more work gets dumped on rural women, they benefit from it—and sometimes not. When Egyptian men emigrated to find work in Libya and the Gulf states, their wives had to take over at home. Along with a heavier workload, the women also gained control over the family resources, which led to new skills, self-confidence, and independence. When Yemeni men emigrated, however, their wives were left under the authority of another male relative or neighbor and had no chance to gain new experience or power.

The Work Forecast

Any discussion of women's work must recognize that workers are increasingly affected by developments far beyond their control or comprehension. A primary factor is economic globalization. Another is the sweeping changes that governments have been undertaking in the past ten years or so to achieve sounder management of their own economies and to meet the requirements of international financial bodies such as the World Bank.

Partly because of these changes, the first years of the twenty-first century see severe economic hardship in many countries, especially unemployment. Even in a country such as Saudi Arabia, long regarded as enormously wealthy, the unemployment rate of young men was officially stated to be 18 percent in 2002. Privileged students in Beirut worry about their job prospects. In a poor country such as Yemen, the unemployment problem is acute. These hardships will certainly affect women's chances in their countries' workforces.

The forecast is therefore full of questions. Will the daughters of today's uneducated women have good chances for jobs—and better lives—tomorrow? Or in times of economic downturn, will patriarchal attitudes reemerge and subject women to harsh discrimination? On another level, will societies in which most women work outside the home run high risks of social problems, or will the traditional focus on the family remain strong enough to meet the challenges?

In any event, it's hard to imagine a significant reversal regarding Middle Eastern women's right to work. They have come too far along the road to greater autonomy and self-expression to ever again be confined to the kitchen.

A policewoman directs traffic in downtown Tunis.

11

Women in the Arts and Athletics

Hands perish, but not their work.

—Arabic proverb

*H*ome and workplace are not the only sites where Middle Eastern women keep busy. Some put in long hours at the writing desk, in the studio, or on the track and court.

A weaver at work on a colorful wall hanging depicting the rural life of Egypt

Writers

Educated women in Egypt and Lebanon started writing in the 1890s, if not earlier, producing more than twenty-five magazines before World War I. These publications featured not just recipes and fashions but discussion of women's issues, openly challenging beliefs and customs that oppressed women. The women's publications contributed to rising political assertiveness in the Arab world, including demand for independence from the Ottoman Empire, which controlled much of the Middle East until 1918.[1]

In the early twentieth century a number of women writers in Egypt held regular gatherings in their elegant homes, attended by the leading intellectuals of the day, male and female. One of the most prominent was May Ziadeh, whose short stories are still admired for their psychological insights.

How was it possible that Middle Eastern women, constrained in so many ways, were free to express themselves in writing? The answer lies in the importance of "the word" since ancient times. Poetry has always been esteemed in Middle Eastern societies, and during the golden age of Islamic civilization, women poets were greatly admired. The traditional respect for learning and literature reemerged in the second half of the nineteenth century.

It was not just educated women, however, who realized the power of the word. Women in traditional societies created their own adventures through storytelling. In the Gulf states such as Kuwait and Qatar, where pearl diving flourished before the discovery of oil, the women would tell each other fantasy tales while the men were away at sea. Elderly women storytellers in Tunis are still popular at women's events such as wedding parties. Their stories in the *Arabian Nights* mode—often quite racy—provide links between the traditional way of life and the rapidly changing present.

Today women writers of North Africa and the Middle East receive ever-increasing international attention. In 1993 a group of women in Cairo founded a publishing house called *Nour* (light), which publishes books by women and a review magazine. In 1995, Nour organized a highly successful first-ever event: the Arab Women's Book Fair, which featured an intense four-day program and hundreds of books written and published by women throughout the region. Plans to hold such fairs regularly have not yet succeeded, unfortunately.

Poets are still greatly esteemed in the Arab/Muslim world. Probably the best-known Iranian woman poet is Forugh Farrokhzad, who died in 1967 at the age of thirty-four. Her poems, banned at the time because of their rebellion against traditional norms and their focus on women's needs and passions, are eagerly read by Iranian girls today.[2]

Women novelists produce much work, often translated into English and other languages, that reveals truths about life in the Middle East in ways that no amount of reporting and scholarly writing could do. Algerian and Moroccan writers were among the first to explore the lives of Muslim women. An early (1964) autobiographical novel by an Algerian is revealingly titled, *Oh, My Muslim Sisters, Weep!* Another inside view comes from Iran, where women writers are creating vivid descriptions to preserve both traditional life and conditions under the Islamic government.[3]

Much literature by Middle Eastern women focuses, almost obsessively, on the struggle of the individual woman to realize her identity and assert her independence within a confining society. Another "revolutionary" theme is woman's right to accept and enjoy her body, traditionally considered a source of shame in Middle Eastern cultures.[4] While some writers utilize fantasy and experimental styles of writing, others give down-to-earth, realistic views of their times. Sahar Khalifeh's novel *Wild Thorns*, both grim and humorous, vividly depicts Palestinians living under Israeli rule.

The long war in Lebanon (1975–1991) inspired much writing by women. Hardly had peace returned to Beirut when a conference was held, in September 1992, on "Arab Women and Literary Creativity," with participants from all over the region. Whereas male writers typically argued about the politics of the war, even glorifying the struggle, women such as Emily Nasrallah and Etel Adnan described the horrors of war in terms of human suffering.[5] The war experience also produced a dramatic change in what women could write about and what the public would accept. In 1964 a young Lebanese woman was taken to court for publishing an "immoral" story, which actually contained only a few mild sexual references. In contrast, a novel published in 1980 about a Muslim woman during wartime graphically described the character's sordid sexual encounters.[6]

As for scholarly works, Arab/Muslim women have distinguished themselves in many fields: political science, history, anthropology, literature, and so forth. A Beirut group called *Bahithat* (Female Researchers) publishes a substantive volume every year. Like creative writers, women scholars write predominantly about women; probably the best known is the Moroccan writer Fatima Mernissi. Sometimes a woman researcher can accomplish more than a man. For instance, a Saudi anthropologist, Mai Yamani, recently surveyed attitudes of Saudi youth; a male researcher would not have had access to the young women, but Yamani talked to both sexes.[7]

Some writers, interested in women's history and heritage before the inroads of Western influence, focus on historical Muslim women. For instance, 'A'isha, wife of the Prophet Muhammad, attracts attention as a role model for modern Arab women.

Artists

As usually interpreted, the Qur'an prohibits depictions of living creatures; therefore, until quite recently most Islamic cultures did not permit the sort of representational pictures familiar in the Western world.[8] Artistic creativity was instead channeled into architecture and crafts—ornate metalwork, inlaid wood, textiles, glassware, ceramics, calligraphy, jewelry—mostly produced by men.

Hala Almaast, fine arts student and Ayyubid architecture specialist from Syria

Women in traditional societies expressed their artistic abilities through weaving and needlecraft. Probably the finest needlework is that of Palestinian women. Their dresses, covered with elaborate, colorful designs, rank among the world's most beautiful ethnic costumes. A recent innovation in needlework is "stitchery pictures" made in Achmeem, Egypt, where women hand-stitch charming scenes of rural life on cloth.

Although even male artists did not gain recognition in the Middle East until the twentieth century, a few Egyptian women became painters decades ago. Effat Nagui was still producing good work in the early 1990s, at the age of ninety-two. Lebanon boasts a vigorous art scene with many galleries, competitions, and painters, such as Helen Khal and Rima Amyuni. Creative women throughout the region are increasingly recognized: an exhibition of women artists' work was held in the United Arab Emirates in 1995.

The first major exhibition of work by Arab women artists—seventy, from fifteen countries—toured the United States in 1993. No quaint peasant scenes or romantic desert views here; rather, much of this contemporary art is intricately abstract or boldly expressive. Especially striking is these artists' concern with contemporary political and social problems. Their paintings and sculptures are protests against poverty, degradation of the environment, torture, oppression of women. They depict young victims of war. Like writers, many women artists challenge the injustices of their societies and call attention to the struggle for a better world.[9]

Musicians

In such countries as Egypt, Lebanon, and Tunisia, middle-class girls have been studying voice and piano for many years. The most talented musicians pursue careers as performers in their own countries and in Europe. Armenians living in Lebanon and Egypt are especially known for their musical and artistic talent. The recently established Lebanese National Symphony includes several Armenian women musicians.

While classical Western music appeals mainly to a small urban audience, the indigenous music of Arab and Persian cultures is immensely popular. Like literature, music and musicians have always held an important place in Middle Eastern cultural life. Classical Arab music is rich and complex. Most instrumentalists are men, but women singers have become almost legendary stars.[10]

Two singers are so popular that they are known by their first names only. One, a Lebanese Christian named Fairouz, has sung her hauntingly beautiful songs for at least fifty years. The other is Egypt's Umm Kulthum, who died in 1975 but is still unquestionably the queen of Arab music. She earned a fortune during her long career, while enhancing the social position of singers by her dignified behavior. The whole Arab world mourned at Umm Kulthum's death.

Lebanese diva Fairouz

Dancers

Although Cairo boasts a ballet company, started in the 1960s with Russian coaches, ballet and modern dance have only a small number of followers, mostly in Lebanon and Egypt. A stunning event on the Iranian cultural scene in the summer of 1998 was the first public performance of modern dance permitted in twenty years. The star was a famous Iranian ballet dancer, Farzaneh Kaboli, long banned from the stage. Held in a school basement, the event was regarded as a large crack in the regime's repression of Western-influenced artistic activity.[11]

Traditional dancing, often called oriental dance, is an enjoyable part of many women's lives. Girls learn this type of dancing at an early age, and women usually dance at women's gatherings such as wedding parties. Professional belly dancers, on the other hand, for which Egypt is famous, are extremely skillful entertainers. Today some serious dancers are promoting oriental dance as a fine art form.[12]

Folk dancing is also popular. Weddings and other celebrations always include dances such as the *debke* of Syria and Lebanon. This is a rhythmic, stamping dance that people do in a line, men and women together, often impromptu. Folk-dancing classes are taught in many countries, from North Africa to the Gulf states, and colorful dance troupes occasionally go on tour. In 1999 a troupe of teenagers from a Palestinian refugee camp near Bethlehem toured the United States. Dance is one of the most vigorous aspects of Middle Eastern culture.

Actors and Filmmakers

The liveliest theater district is in Cairo, although such cities as Beirut and Tunis also have several theaters that produce plays—often avant-garde satire and social criticism—by

Middle Eastern playwrights. As for popular cinema, Egyptian films are the best known in the Arab world. They feature broad comedy, dashing historical pieces, and tear-jerking melodramas, all of which allow Egyptian actresses to perform with lavish displays of emotion.

Serious filmmaking is now one of the most exciting of all art forms in the Middle East and lends itself to the talents of women directors and producers. Increasingly, female film-makers—Palestinian, Lebanese, Iranian, Tunisian, Egyptian—are getting well-deserved international attention. Many films, whether made by women or men, focus on women's lives in brutally honest fashion, exploring character and relationships much more revealingly than a Hollywood treatment would allow. Women filmmakers don't flinch from subjects usually avoided in their society, such as homosexuality, as well as political problems.[13]

Runners and Walkers

In Western and some Asian countries, athletics is another field where women have a chance both to excel and to earn a living. Thus far, however, that has not been true in the Middle East. Sports for women—especially highly competitive sports—are a recent development in the area, too new to produce many outstanding athletes on the international sports scene.

The talent is undoubtedly there, however, waiting for adequate training and the money to compete in important international events. A few countries, notably Morocco, Algeria, and Syria, have sent strong women runners to major international competitions, including the Olympics, and these women have brought back medals. In 1993 the first Islamic Women's Games, a revolutionary sports event, was held in Tehran, Iran. Muslim women from all over Asia and much of Africa competed in track, swimming, shooting, table tennis, volleyball, and other events, wearing shorts and swimsuits before an exclusively female audience.[14] The success of the event led to a second Islamic Women's Games in 1997, also in Tehran, and discussions for future all-female Islamic Olympics.

Team sports are highly popular in most countries, especially basketball and volleyball. Girls play these sports in high schools just about everywhere, and at some universities. At the University of Jordan, a basketball game between girls' teams—many of the players in hijab—will pack the gymnasium with wildly cheering students, more men than women! Often an informal game of men's pickup basketball at the American University of Beirut will include a couple of girls.

In North Africa, women's basketball and volleyball teams reach an almost professional level. Tunisian cities all have at least one volleyball team, sponsored by various businesses. They play against teams from around the country and with champion teams from other African countries. Players start training as young as twelve years old and compete into their thirties.

Egypt, where soccer is played and cheered with passion, now has a national team for women. It took years to overcome resistance in that conservative country: soccer would expose women's legs and "ruin their virginity." But thanks to the efforts of one young woman, daughter of a soccer coach, the team was finally launched in 1997.[15]

Although competitive athletics are possible for only a very few women, fitness activities are becoming more common for all ages. At sporting clubs in Cairo, for instance, boys and girls practice karate together, and middle-aged women can be seen on the lawns doing stretching exercises with men. (The women do *not* wear shorts.) In the segregated society of Saudi Arabia and some Gulf states, women take fitness and dance classes in private clubs. The beaches near Casablanca in Morocco get lots of female jogging traffic. In Beirut, every morning women in smart jogging suits speed-walk along the seaside promenade; in the evenings they get their husbands and boyfriends out walking with them.

For most Middle Eastern women, however, exercise for the sake of health and enjoyment is an expense they can't afford. Parks and other places where people can exercise in safe surroundings are hard to find in most of the over-crowded, unplanned cities of the region. Conservative attitudes in small towns and villages would discourage walking or running in sports clothing. And for the innumerable women who work long hours in the home, fields, or factories, there's no time or energy left over for recreational exercise, even if it were available.

Young couples rest following an afternoon jog along Beirut's Corniche.

12

Women in Public Life

Intelligence is the ornament of every serious woman.
—Lebanese proverb

When you speak, do not fear; when you fear, do not speak.
—Iraqi proverb

*I*n the patriarchal societies of the Middle East, how active a public role can women play? This chapter will look at two ways in which women are trying to make themselves heard and to affect the course of events: the peaceful processes of political participation and vigorous, even violent, confrontation.

Women in the Political Process

It's often—but misleadingly—argued that there are no democracies in the Arab/Muslim world. While no government comes close to those of Western nations, and while elections typically fall far short of appropriate standards, the majority of states have elected parliaments and local governments. And in most countries, women have the right to vote.

Turkey was the leader, granting women the vote in 1934. Syria came next, in 1949; and Lebanon, in 1953. In some cases women's suffrage was achieved along with revolutionary changes in government. Egypt granted women voting rights in 1956, four years after a radical socialist government took over. Two of the North African countries formerly colonized by France allowed women to vote soon after independence: Tunisia in 1956 and Algeria in 1962. Morocco waited until 1963, seven years after independence.

Only in Saudi Arabia and the Gulf states are women denied the ballot. In most of those countries no one can vote, because the system of government is either a traditional one without democratically elected bodies or highly authoritarian.

The struggle for women's suffrage in Kuwait, where certain classes of men can vote, is a special story. In 1990, when Iraq invaded Kuwait, many Kuwaiti women—who could have fled the country—stayed to help resist the foreign occupiers. They smuggled documents and arms under their cloaks, kept hospitals functioning, even sabotaged Iraqi military vehicles. Many were imprisoned, tortured, and killed. Having gained international recognition for their efforts, they hoped to be granted voting rights after the liberation of Kuwait in 1991.

Sadly, the patriarchal society reemerged as strong as ever. Women were told to go home and forget about politics. Instead, many Kuwaiti women have repeatedly demonstrated and petitioned to become first-class citizens. In 1999 a decree by the Emir (hereditary ruler of Kuwait) granting women the right to vote and hold office was killed by the parliament. The Emir has promised women political rights for the next elections, in 2003, and in the meantime, progressive women are keeping up the pressure.[1]

Women's experience in being elected to legislative bodies unfortunately reflects their status in the social order. In Jordan, for instance, tribal and patriarchal attitudes are still a major obstacle. The first woman to serve in Jordan's parliament, Toujan Feisel, was elected in 1993 after an intense campaign, but did not survive the next election. In Egypt, where an increasingly authoritarian regime has dampened public enthusiasm for the political process, the number of female members of parliament has declined from a high of 35 (out of 454) in 1984 to only 11 elected in 2000.

But success comes in small steps. Two of those eleven women came from the conservative southern part of Egypt, which suggests that men *can* support female candidates.[2] In Lebanon, three women have served in the last two elected parliaments (1996 and 2000). While they owed their presence to connections with powerful male figures, they have proved hard-working and effective.[3] Local Lebanese elections in 1998 saw 140 women elected to municipal councils, largely because of personal qualifications rather than family connections as in the past.[4] Women candidates have been elected to the Iranian parliament since 1992 and they look forward eventually to being able to speak with a strong voice.[5] In September 2002, Morocco set a new standard for the whole region, reserving thirty seats for women (10 percent) in parliamentary elections.

Governments appoint very few women to ministerial positions. When they do, it is almost always a ministry "appropriate" for women, such as social welfare or culture. On the other hand, in a culture where who you are counts for a great deal, first ladies can push social and political agendas. Jordan's young queen, Rania, speaks effectively for women's issues. Suzanne Mubarak, wife of Egypt's president, has long supported libraries for children and now heads the National Council for Women (founded in 2000), an organization concerned with women's rights.

To persuade women to vote and run for office—and to persuade men to lower the barriers—will take continuing effort. Regional and international conferences keep the issue alive. Given Western experience, where women's political rights were won only after arduous struggle in the twentieth century and where women are still underrepresented in government, it's not surprising that Middle Eastern society is slow to get women involved in political decision making.

Queen Rania speaks at the Arab Women's Summit in December 2001.

Women on the Front Lines

In the early days of Islam, Arab women fought in battle along with the men, and epic poems celebrated female warriors. In the twentieth century the walls that had been set up to protect women began to crumble. Egyptian women demonstrated in the streets against British colonial rule in 1919, which launched Middle Eastern women into active roles in political events.

Algeria

After France conquered Algeria in the 1830s and colonized the land with European settlers, the Muslim inhabitants suffered from severe poverty and discrimination. A national liberation war broke out in 1954 and raged for eight years.

During this brutal war as many as 10,000 women and girls helped to fight for Algerian independence. Most played supporting roles, such as preparing food for the fighters, but other women transported arms beneath their veils and robes, carried messages and documents, and even fought alongside the men. Some young women made their way through the streets of Algiers with bombs in their purses, knowing they could die with the intended victims or be arrested and tortured. This active role in warfare was all the more remarkable in light of the extremely restricted lives that Algerian women had led traditionally.[6]

They had every reason to expect that a free Algeria would bring major improvements in their lives. But with Algeria's independence the patriarchal structure came to life again. In 1984 the government adopted a comprehensive family law that destroyed any semblance of equality between men and women, decreeing that women have the status of minors for their entire lives, under the control of husband or kinsman. Women demonstrated against it, with no success.

In 1992, Islamist extremists started fighting against the national government, using terrorism as a weapon. Leaders of Algerian women's groups were targeted for assassination along with teachers, journalists, and intellectuals—a time of horror depicted in Assia Djebar's novel *Algerian White* (2001). Wives and daughters of government employees were warned to wear the veil and stay at home—or be killed.[7] Algerian professors with whom the author (EM) spoke in Tunis said they lived in constant fear of death.

Dismayed but defiant, Algerian women protested. For example, in 1994 a large crowd of women carried a banner through the streets of Algiers calling for freedom of expression, even in the face of death threats.[8] While the situation in Algeria was calmer by the early 2000s, backlash against women by extremist groups continues to be a matter of concern.

Lebanon

From 1975 to 1991 the small country of Lebanon was torn by an immensely complicated and destructive war, involving many different armies and militias. The war brought terrible hardship, but also new opportunities, for Lebanese women.

Military training in Baghdad

The most striking tradition-breakers were those young women who joined militias, fighting along with the men in the streets. The great majority, possibly thousands, served in a large Christian militia called the Lebanese Forces. In 1987 it formed a military academy, and at their insistence, women militia members were trained in exactly the same way as the men. Unlike many men who joined militias for a variety of reasons, the women fought for patriotic motives and were intensely committed to their cause.[9]

Other women helped their "militia of choice" by cooking for the fighters and tending the wounded. Among the Muslims and Druze (a close-knit Muslim sect with a reputation as tough fighters), women were not allowed to take part in battles. It was feared that they might be captured and very possibly raped, which would be a shame to their families. Nonetheless, Muslim women were known for their bravery, especially in southern Lebanon. When the Israeli army invaded Lebanon in 1982, these women often openly confronted the soldiers.[10]

Women also worked in organizations that helped the hundreds of thousands of civilian victims. Girls drove ambulances into battle, transporting the wounded to hospitals. One proudly described her experiences to the author (EM). "I stayed in the back part of the ambulance with the wounded people, and when militiamen tried to hold us up, I would stick my head out and shout at them. I was *strong!*"

The traditional respect for women—even though it may be based on the assumption that they are unimportant—can literally save lives. Sometimes, to get what they needed for their families, women made demands on the military forces that controlled their neighborhoods. Their husbands, acting in the same way, probably would not have lived to tell about it. For example, an unmarried, middle-aged woman was stopped by some Syrian soldiers while driving. They got in and ordered her to take them somewhere—a common sort of incident. "I can't take you," she said coolly. "My husband wouldn't like it. Would you like it if a strange man got into your wife's car with her?" The men thought it over. "You're right," they said, and got out.[11]

Not least was the bravery of thousands of ordinary women. Deprived of their husbands and sons, they were forced to learn roles and skills entirely new to them, often in such dangerous conditions that just getting water was a life-or-death challenge.[12]

Palestinian Women

Palestinians'efforts to achieve an independent state have involved violence, as most resistance movements do. Women's roles, however, have been characterized by a different strategy: organization.

Palestinian women have a long history of organized activity, starting in 1929 with charitable projects led by socially prominent individuals. In the late 1970s younger women with more radical aims established new organizations that focused both on political matters and on projects affecting women, such as literacy classes, nurseries, and health issues. More important, they mobilized women of all classes and in all parts of the Palestinian territories.

Palestinian women protesting actions by Israeli military forces.

In November 1987 the first Palestinian *intifada* broke out, a popular uprising against the occupying military forces of Israel. The women's committees, experienced in organizing people and providing services, quickly took leadership roles. As the Israeli army tried to put down the uprising the local women's groups got to work. They taught first aid, knit sweaters for men held in prison, and encouraged community solidarity by supporting families of people killed or imprisoned. "Ordinary" women became active, in some villages as leaders.[13]

Women also got directly involved in confrontations. Grandmothers rushed into the street to protect boys from Israeli soldiers. Teenage girls also took an active part in resistance. In spite of the traditional emphasis on shame and honor, families came to take pride in daughters and wives who underwent imprisonment and harsh interrogation.[14]

The years from 1994 to 2000 brought a so-called peace process, agreed upon by Israeli and Palestinian leaders; one of the prominent Palestinian negotiators was a woman, Hanan Ashrawi, a professor and writer. During that period, however, the Israeli army remained firmly in control of Palestinian territory and Palestinian lives, and illegal settlements of Israelis on Palestinian land grew faster than ever. In September 2000 a second intifada broke out, leading to intense struggle between Palestinian resistance fighters and the Israeli army, government, and settlers.

In this uprising, women have not played a prominent role. Under military assault almost daily, they can focus only on the safety of their families and the neighborhood children.[15] Some Palestinian women living in Israel participate with Israeli peace groups in protesting the actions of the Israeli government and army; but at the time of writing, no resolution to this horrific conflict is in sight.

A Middle Eastern woman who takes a stand publicly for her convictions requires unflinching courage and commitment. Her actions affect not just herself, but her whole family and her husband's reputation. Yet, though the ranks are still small, women are stepping into the front lines, in many instances leading the struggle for changes that must come to their societies sooner or later.

CHAPTER 13

Is There a Middle Eastern Women's Movement?

*If you are an anvil, be patient; but if you are
a hammer, strike!*

—Arabic proverb

*G*iven the great diversity in this huge region, naturally there has been no one unified women's movement but rather a mobilizing of women in each country at different times and in different ways. Only in the last twenty years or so have women started working together through conferences and sharing of research.

Women's Organizations (NGOs)

As in Western societies, a women's movement logically starts with volunteer organizations. In Middle Eastern societies, the role of nongovernmental organizations (referred to as NGOs) is vital. They play all sorts of roles that governments either do not handle or cannot deal with as well as a citizens' group could. In some countries, NGOs proliferate to the point of competition and confusion.

Women's charitable organizations, often connected with religious institutions, started in Egypt in the nineteenth century and in such countries as Lebanon and Palestine, early in the twentieth century. There are still many of this sort. They run kindergartens, give literacy classes, provide clerical training, teach about hygiene, organize self-help projects, and so on. This is a natural way to extend women's traditional role as caregiver, the "proper" sort of thing for women to do in the public sphere.

Other women's NGOs focus more on specific interests, such as business and professional associations. Many have objectives such as environmental concerns or support for a certain hospital, orphanage, or school.

In several countries there are goverment-sponsored national women's organizations that are allowed to tackle some problems that affect women. For instance, the Women's Union in Syria pushed through a national requirement that employers provide nurseries for female workers' children, and the General Federation of Iraqi Women worked on a successful project to provide classes for girls who have to drop out of school. In these tightly controlled societies, however, women's unions are virtually support groups for government objectives.[1]

Women attend a gathering to discuss women's rights in Afghanistan.

Jordan and Tunisia also have official women's unions. The Jordanian one is an umbrella organization for many societies that carry on charitable and educational work. Some women see these organizations as too cautious and support other groups with more radical programs.[2]

Saudi Arabia has private charitable groups concerned with women's health, family needs, and so forth but no organizations concerned with social issues or women's rights. In contrast, since the 1950s women in Bahrain have had active societies with a strong public and political focus. Several women's organizations exist in Kuwait and the United Arab Emirates, largely for charitable and cultural activities but also concerned with some social problems.

In some countries women have organized to tackle controversial and sensitive matters, in addition to political awareness. They promote family planning; they campaign against honor crimes, female genital mutilation, domestic violence, and abuse of imported domestic workers. In Algeria and Morocco, they do something that was unthinkable ten or fifteen years ago: maintain shelters for unwed mothers, homeless women, and young girls who have run away from intolerable conditions.[3] The outstanding Lebanese activist Laure Moghaizel, a lawyer and leader in numerous organizations, was concerned with women's issues and human rights until her death in 1997.

To conclude this brief survey, let us look at two very different projects undertaken by Egyptian women. The Arab Women's Solidarity Association was founded in Cairo in 1982 by Nawal el-Saadawi, doubtless the most influential feminist leader and writer in the whole region. In 1986 the association held a conference attended by prominent scholars and activists from many Arab countries. But when members later criticized government policy too freely, the Egyptian government disbanded it. This organization was clearly ahead of its time.

The second enterprise was the Egyptian Women's Health Book Collective. Twenty-two women from different fields of study, social classes, and age groups produced a book inspired by one published in the United States, *Our Bodies, Ourselves*. Carefully tailored to its audience and well received, the Egyptian book provided objective information on controversial subjects while avoiding topics still taboo, a good example of what an organization can do when well focused.[4]

Women's Studies

The second phase of a women's movement is to learn more about the subject—women—and to make that information available. To this end, several institutes or programs have been established in the Middle East, starting with the pioneering Institute for Women's Studies in the Arab World (1973) at the Lebanese American University in Beirut. IWSAW conducts research, publishes an outstanding English-language periodical concerned with women's issues (*Al-Raida*, "The Pioneer"), and sponsors conferences, film festivals, photo exhibits, and so forth.

Birzeit University, a Palestinian university in the West Bank, has an interdisciplinary Women's Studies Institute, founded in 1994, to carry out and publish research, primarily on Palestinian women. It offers courses and degrees at the undergraduate and graduate levels. Typically, half of those enrolled in the introductory courses are young men, some genuinely interested and some looking to challenge the ideas being discussed.[5]

Two vigorous organizations in Tunisia are the Center for Research, Study, Documentation, and Information on Women (CREDIF) and the Center of Arab Women for Training and Research (CAWTAR). In Istanbul, the New Women's Library is a documentation center on Turkish women.

Afghan women participate in a women's conference sponsored by the United Nations and the Afghan Women's Association.

An Institute for Gender and Women's Studies at the American University in Cairo carries on research, conferences, and policy debates. In 2001 a center for women's studies opened at Tehran University, after a seven-year campaign by Iranian female professors.[6]

Yemen has women's studies centers at the University of Aden and at the University of Sana'a. The latter has a student enrollment about half male. "Men still control public life," says one of the instructors. "They are the decision makers, so we need to involve men in understanding women's issues."[7] And there are other centers—all told, a far cry from the outmoded assumption that women's lives were not worth much scrutiny.

Women's Movements of Special Interest

Every effort of women to work for progress in their societies and in their own lives deserves attention. Some naturally are better documented than others, and some are particularly problematic.

The women's movement in Egypt is doubtless the best known. Its founder, Hoda Sha'rawi, led the first pro-nationalist demonstrations by women and is probably most celebrated for publicly discarding her face veil in 1923 as a symbolic gesture. From then on, with relentless effort, Egyptian women achieved numerous milestones. National unions were founded, and even a women's political party (Daughters of the Nile, 1948). The first female cabinet minister was appointed in 1962. Egyptian women played an active role in the 1994 International Conference on Population and Development held in Cairo and took part in the Beijing Conference for Women's Development (1995).[8] They still have many battles to wage.

In the case of Palestinian women, we have seen how they participated in the first intifada (1987–1992) by developing an organizational network. Later, however, the movement weakened, and the traditional patriarchy of conservative Palestinian society reasserted itself.

Here, then, is the dilemma that Palestinian women face. Palestinians' overriding objective is freedom from military occupation and domination by Israel, and ultimately an independent, viable Palestinian state. For several years, therefore, activist women have asked, Do we push *now* for greater political participation and significantly improved women's rights, which might weaken the movement for statehood by bringing up divisive issues? Or do we put all our energies into the nationalist goal and sometime later on work toward our own goals? Palestinian women are all too aware of what happened to women in Algeria following that country's independence.

Palestinian women demonstrate in Lebanon on March 8, 2002, International Women's Day.

In the 1990s the Palestinian political leadership made clear that women were not wanted in governing circles—even though, paradoxically, one of the most prominent and respected spokespersons for the Palestinian cause is a woman, Hanan Ashrawi. Women's role has been officially described only as supporters of men.[9]

The picture is full of contradiction. Educated women, angry and frustrated at being pushed aside, continue to work with political parties, research centers, and human rights groups. But other women, especially the impoverished and uneducated, are resigned to a very subservient role. In a few refugee camps women's centers offer a chance to learn, explore alternative ways of thinking, and share experiences without fear.[10] But they are working against extremely conservative attitudes, reinforced by the Islamist movement, which grows stronger with the continuing conflict. This is partly because under the conditions of the Israeli occupation, many Palestinian men have only one thing left with which to assert their traditional ideas of dignity and honor: a heavy hand over women.

The challenge to Palestinian women, therefore, involves both resolution of the political conflict and basic changes in ways of thinking. Yet their strength lies in their superior education, experience in organization and mobilization, and possibly the best connection to the world at large—through the Internet—of any national group of Middle Eastern women. Their story, despite its many frustrations, may provide inspiration and an example for women in other societies.

Iran's women also have an interesting recent history. Under the long rule of the shah (1941–1979), they made enormous advances in education, political rights, personal freedoms, employment, and professional distinction. But the shah's government grew despotic, and a revolution led to its overthrow early in 1979. At that time, tens of thousands of women marched in often bloody demonstrations against the shah. Encouraged by this experience, women then demonstrated in support of the revolutionary Islamic regime—and later, when the new government in turn became repressive, against it. In March 1979, over 15,000 women took to the streets of Tehran to protest the revolutionary government's attack on women's rights.

Under the new regime, women lost their positions in government and their equal chance at education and employment. The Family Protection Law was rescinded, and cruel punishments decreed for various crimes. All women were forced to wear the hijab, and bands of "morals police" enforced rules requiring segregation of the sexes.

But with their education and previous experience, Iranian women didn't take it lying down. They could still write, petition, and voice their demands, and they did so. Nor were these mainly the Westernized elite who spoke out but rather strongly religious women from the lower middle class who supported the idea of an Islamic society and took pride in revived Islamic culture. Appealing to religious principles, they forced the government to back off from its extreme policies. Thus the Islamic government, by trying to banish women from active public life, instead created an effective new voice of protest.[11]

By the 1990s, Iranian women were back solidly in the university, government office, and workplace. Many became family breadwinners, because their husbands, associated with the shah's regime, had lost their jobs. Women's organizations were once more in favor, with several official agencies focused on women's affairs.

Popular reaction to the dress code perhaps best reveals the government's inability to clamp down forever on women's behavior. Today, not only can colorful scarves, locks of hair, and glimpses of fashionable clothes be seen under the chador but even the holes-at-the-knees jeans of teenagers and "cool" bulky sweaters instead of the required drab overcoat. Women are very much involved in political demonstrations, for instance against persecution of political dissidents, and female students speak openly of the need for political change.[12]

The climate in Iran is certainly not yet free. But a summing-up of the women's movement there would perhaps go something like this: once women have had the opportunity to see better lives for themselves, they will be hard to keep down for long. And if they know how to "fight fire with fire," as Islamic feminists do in basing their claims on Islam, they can win their rights.

But Is This Islamic Feminism?

In the mid-1990s, Elizabeth Fernea, an American scholar with long experience in the Middle East and North Africa, undertook a tour of several countries from Morocco to Iraq. She sought an understanding of how women in these predominantly Muslim countries see themselves as they work to bring about change in their societies. She heard Moroccan women proudly explain how they pressured the king to make substantive changes in the family law in

1992[13] and heard Saudi women assert that "Saudization" of the workforce would indeed include Saudi women. She joined in intellectual discussion at elegant gatherings in Kuwait, and in Turkey accompanied women taking toys to the children of the very poor.

Would all this activity directed at improving women's lives be called feminism? And if so, Fernea asked her many contacts, would you call it Islamic feminism? The answers ranged from annoyance to perplexity and did not lead to a clear conclusion. Whether a woman activist in the Middle East chooses to call herself a feminist, it seems, is a matter of personal choice.

On one thing, however, most Middle Eastern feminists agreed: they don't want to be forced into the mold of Western feminism. They reject the extremes that some Western feminists went to in the past, demanding equality with men, even to the point of imitating the worst things about male behavior, while belittling the domestic role of wife and mother. They don't seek a society in which men and women are separated by distrust and competition but rather a society in which women and men play complementary, sometimes shared, roles based on mutual respect. And they don't want Western feminists telling them what they should do. They want to find their own solutions, within the framework of their own societies and values.

Many women who have asserted their desire for a society based on Islamic principles would not dream of retiring to their kitchens and nurseries. Devout Muslims and Islamists, they see their role as very much in the world—studying, working at whatever occupation they wish, continuing the struggle to bring about a better society for people of all classes. That, they believe, is what Islam is all about, and they can quote the Qur'an and the Prophet to back up what they say.[14]

14

A Woman's Later Years

*A house without an elderly person is like
an orchard without a well.*
—Arabic proverb

When a woman passes beyond her childbearing years, her status in the traditional Middle Eastern family changes—usually for the better. No longer does she need the protection that younger women do. A previously jealous husband may relax the limitations he puts on her. In the public eye an older woman doesn't need to worry about the attentions of strange men and, therefore, can move about more freely. This transition doubtless produces mixed emotions in many an older woman.

Authority with Age

A major change occurs once a woman becomes a mother-in-law. The mother-son relationship is typically very strong; indeed, a man's mother is often the only woman with whom he feels comfortable expressing his emotions.[1] A son's strong loyalty to his mother is an enduring feature of the Middle Eastern family.

Predictably, this closeness can lead to tensions when the son brings home a bride. A mother may try to hold on to her son's affection by interfering in his relationship with his wife.

As the senior woman of the household, she expects to dominate her new daughter-in-law, and the younger woman is expected to submit. In a traditional Moroccan household, for instance, the mother-in-law keeps the key to the storage room where food and staples are kept. Her daughter-in-law must ask permission to obtain whatever she needs. When the son buys something for his wife, by tradition he should get the same for his mother.

Little wonder, then, that Middle Eastern folktales and movies are full of mothers-in-law who browbeat and overwork their sons' wives! Mother-in-law conflict is one of the main factors contributing to divorce.

Despite the stereotypes, however, the mother-in-law can be a friend and teacher for her son's wife. Because traditional husbands aren't encouraged to communicate openly with their wives, the wife may look to her mother-in-law for companionship. "A good woman! God bless her memory," says one elderly Palestinian of her mother-in-law. "She taught me to cook and bake. . . . I swear, it was a good life in those days."[2]

Another positive role for the older woman is that of grandmother, much loved and respected. As bearer of tradition, a grandmother is sought after for advice and wisdom. Her presence in the home reminds younger members of a time before television, when families spent more time together and knew the dances and stories of their people better than they do today.

As a woman ages, she is freed from the heavier tasks and usually spends more time on food preparation. In rural Yemen a choice job is reserved for the older woman: for three or four hours every day, she hand-feeds the cows sorghum stalks wrapped in alfalfa.[3] Many village women who have worked hard all their lives have no desire to admit they no longer can work. Seasonal tasks such as harvesting olives mark a rural woman's year, and older women may suffer emotionally when forced to give them up.

Even though no longer vigorous, an older woman now has time to devote to matchmaking, visiting, and teaching the younger family members. She enjoys an enlarged role in family and community decision making. Since wives tend to outlive their husbands, many households are headed by widows, who may carry full authority over the extended family.

Changing Times, Scattered Families

Yet the advantages of the older woman in an extended family are fading. With families moving toward smaller, nuclear households, older women may find themselves living alone. Although they can still count on their sons for support, it is hard for people brought up in the old ways to adjust to isolation.

The author (RH) talked with an Iranian woman who has found a happy balance in the transition to modern family life. Madame Fatimah, a retired office manager, lives alone in Tehran, but her sons and their families live in the same apartment complex and spend several hours with her every day. Madame Fatimah's present life appears quite traditional, but she doesn't take it for granted: she knows she is lucky.

Another factor adding to the loneliness of elderly women is emigration. Children and grandchildren go abroad for further education, and many don't return. Many men from poor or economically stressed places—Egypt, Lebanon, the Palestinian territories, Algeria—emigrate to find work. Thus the family breaks up further.

Nowhere in the Middle East has the isolation of the elderly reached the levels it has in the West. Family and neighborhood ties still provide support and companionship, and the elderly are still valued for their wisdom. Yet many people wonder, as social and economic changes increasingly disrupt traditional living patterns, how much longer families will be able to care for their older members.

Health

As everywhere, aging women must contend with worsening health. The stresses of multiple pregnancies and poor nutrition take a heavy toll in bent bones and toothless mouths, a common sight in villages.

Where modern health care is expensive, if available at all, older women may just "wait till the pain goes away." Poor people throughout much of the Middle East turn to folk healers. Older women are often experts in the practice of alternative health care and herbal healing, passed down through the generations. Midwives are also powerful figures in many rural communities. Even if a midwife's methods are not always sanitary, her presence as an older woman with much experience inspires confidence.

Tomorrow's Elderly

Homes for the aged, run both by governments and by religious charitable organizations, are relatively uncommon in the Middle East. Family honor still dictates that the infirm be taken care of at home, usually in the household of the oldest son. If hospital stays are necessary, family members typically sit day and night with their sick relative. Except as a last resort, it is considered unfortunate, even shameful, for a family to send an elderly person to a nursing home. But here, too, times are changing. There are more than a dozen homes for the elderly in Lebanon, for example, and more families are becoming willing—or are forced—to take this step.[4]

Nursing homes for the aged, although not common, serve an increasing need in the Middle East.

A promising alternative got under way in Egypt in 1996. The "Care With Love" program trains home-health-care providers, young men as well as women. After a two-year course, graduates are prepared to take care of infirm people in the home setting. This project offers hope of a good alternative to long, unpleasant, and expensive hospital stays, and should raise the status of health-care givers.[5]

Middle Eastern populations have a high percentage of children and youths. But statistics show that people are living longer, thanks to better health and medical treatment. In 1990 the average life expectancy for women in the Middle East (not counting North Africa) was approximately sixty-three years. By 2000 it had increased to sixty-eight years, and in 2010 it is projected to be seventy-one years. (Men's life expectancy seems to stay a steady three years shorter than women's.)[6] At the same time that older women are living longer, successful family planning programs will mean fewer babies. The future, therefore, will find more elderly women with fewer young people to take care of them—the same situation as in many economically advanced countries.

This forecast demands far-reaching changes in government services and social attitudes. Women's health will have to improve at all stages of life, and women must learn how to take care of themselves. Middle Eastern society faces several changes affecting the aging population: weakening and dispersal of the extended family, fewer family caregivers due to smaller family size and women's employment, and increasing numbers of elderly people requiring care. It's evident that women's need for greater independence, well into their later years, must bring changes in the patriarchal way of thinking.

The Last Rite of Passage

As used to be common in the West, a widow is traditionally expected to wear black, often for a period of years. Her social activities are also reduced, but she does not suffer a serious loss of status in her family or community.

When death comes to a community, it is often older women who take the lead in mourning. In Egyptian villages, hired women mourners are an important part of funerals. Men usually remain reserved at funeral processions, while women are more expressive, wailing and pouring dust on their heads to symbolize their grief. The dead person is carried to the cemetery and, according to Muslim practice, buried before sundown of the day of death. Later, the family receives condolence visits.

Bedouin women in the Western Desert of Egypt compose haunting laments to express their sense of loss:

> O loved one, what you've broken in me,
> Sixty thousand years will not mend. . . .[7]

The ties that bind are felt keenly in the Middle East. Although death is accepted as part of life, it always comes as a shock—and perhaps most to women, whose lives are so intimately bound to the people around them.

Chapter 15

Afghanistan: The Extremes of Oppression

If women are going outside with fashionable, ornamental, tight and charming clothes to show themselves, they will be cursed by the Islamic Sharia and should never expect to go to heaven.

—Decree of the Taliban, November 1996, Kabul [1]

From the late 1970s on, women in Afghanistan endured ever-worsening conditions until, under the Taliban government, they were forced to stay inside their houses day and night. No school, no jobs, virtually no rights whatsoever. How did such extreme oppression come about?

First, a few words on its geopolitical setting. In western Asia, Afghanistan is bounded by Iran, Pakistan, and the Central Asian countries that were formerly part of the Soviet Union. Thanks to its strategic location, it was coveted by the nineteenth-century imperialist powers Russia and Britain; but the Afghans, a fiercely independent people, managed to hold them off and retain a fair degree of autonomy.

Afghan Women in the Twentieth Century

In the 1920s, under a king who promoted progressive reforms, urban Afghan women increasingly experienced modern life. The first school for girls opened in 1921, and women in the ruling family demanded education and recognition of women's abilities.[2] By midcentury, the educated classes in the cities, especially the capital, Kabul, were adopting Western dress and sending their daughters to school. The first women students attended Kabul University in 1950 and the medical college in 1953. Many girls from well-to-do families went abroad for higher education.

Gradually, educated urban women moved into the professions, such as law and medicine. By the 1960s, Afghan women were being appointed to important posts in government and were attending international conferences. The constitution, written in 1964, gave women the vote, and two women served in Afghanistan's senate. A number of women worked on newspapers and edited magazines.

To be sure, at least 90 percent of the population were still villagers or nomads, bound by their traditional ways and little affected by modernization. Yet those women who were educated were playing an important role in their country's progress. Many led lives much like their counterparts in other Middle Eastern capitals—until the 1970s.

The Coming of Chaos

In 1978, after five years of an authoritarian regime, the Communist Party of Afghanistan took power. They undertook some reforms, including women's rights; but change had never proceeded in Afghanistan without strong resistance, especially from conservative religious leaders, and civil order soon broke down. In December 1979 troops of the Soviet Union invaded Afghanistan.

Outside powers now saw Afghanistan, in an oil-rich region, as a critical battlefield in the cold war between the Western democracies and the Communist world. Armed and funded by various countries, including the United States, resistance fighters—*mujahhideen*—took on the Soviet army in a brutal war. Finally the Soviets gave up, and the last Soviet soldiers left in 1989.

In a devastated country still full of weaponry, the mujahhideen now turned both on each other and on the government. Several factions, under "warlords" who commanded tribal and ethnic groupings, fought among themselves, reducing much of Afghanistan's major cities to rubble. Countless women became victims of imprisonment, rape, torture, violent death, and decrees drastically limiting their basic rights.[3] The warlords so weakened each other, demoralized the population, and ruined the country that in 1994 yet another army could move into the picture with relative ease. This was the Taliban, a force based on Islamist ideas.

By autumn of 1996, the Taliban had taken Kabul and controlled much of the country. For a few months people were hopeful. "They were Muslim," an Afghan refugee told the author (EM), "and at first people thought they would be all right." Indeed, the name by which they called themselves, Taliban, means "students" and suggests enlightened people. Before long, however, the Taliban's true colors showed.

Living with the Taliban

One of the Taliban's first actions was to shut the girls' schools. Girls were told to stay at home, and all the women teachers suddenly found themselves out of a job. This affected not only girls but boys, because 70 percent of all elementary school teachers were women. The whole system of education virtually collapsed.

All women who worked outside their homes—about 40 percent of Kabul's women—were forced to give up their jobs and stay at home. The one exception was certain medical personnel, who were allowed to work in hospitals on a strictly gender-segregated basis. With sharply reduced incomes and ever-rising prices, people had to sell everything they could. Many women had no husband or other male family member as breadwinner, because so many men had been killed in the fighting or thrown in prison. These women and their children quickly sank into dire poverty.

No longer could women even go to public bathhouses. Women's homes became their prison. The house windows were painted over, reinforcing women's exclusion from the world outside.

On the rare occasions when she did go out, each woman had to be concealed in a full-length garment commonly known as the *burka*. The burka covers a woman completely, head to toe, with a small patch of less dense material in front of her face. A traditional garment, it is still worn regularly in conservative areas; but for women who would never have worn any kind of hijab, it was an insult. The burka severely restricted the wearer's vision—a hazard on streets full of erratic traffic—and caused physical problems such as hearing loss and skin rashes. Probably worst of all was psychological damage. As an American relief worker said, "When you only see women in burkas, you realize the power of covering a woman like that. You don't treat them like people anymore, just bits of cloth moving down the street."[4]

Even inside a burka, a woman had to have a male escort from her family every time she went out or risk being beaten. Beatings were routine for the slightest offense—if a woman's hand showed or her shoes made noise. In their efforts to create a pious Islamic society, the Taliban set up a Department of the Promotion of Virtue and Prevention of Vice. Thousands of men and teenage boys were authorized to roam the

An Afghan guard takes women prisoners to the court in Herat.

streets, beating any woman in whom they detected a symptom of vice, such as white socks or noisy shoes.

The Taliban degraded, imprisoned, and virtually denied the existence of women. But they still needed the female sex. Girls could be taken by force from their homes and given to Taliban men as "wives," never to be seen or heard from again.

Who Were the Taliban?

In Afghanistan, a country full of ethnic diversity, traditionally Islam was tolerant of other religions and lifestyles.[5] Parts of southern Afghanistan, however, remained rigidly conservative and patriarchal, particularly some of the Pashtun tribe. There the status of women was very low and modern education all but unknown. And that's where the Taliban had their roots. Of the men in leadership positions, virtually none appear to have had any modern education. They came to their jobs equipped with their fighting experience, a totally distorted understanding of their religion, and no notion whatever of how to run a country.[6]

As for the troops, tens of thousands were drawn from youths who had attended religious schools, called *madrassas*, in neighboring Pakistan. A great many were destitute Afghan refugees, orphaned by the long years of warfare.

The madrassas, which had started in a movement to reform and "purify" the religion, were supported in the 1980s by the government of Pakistan, with backing from the United States and Saudi Arabia. Given a free hand, they grew enormously in numbers and power. The quality of education declined, however, until it meant little more than memorizing the Qur'an in Arabic—which the boys did not understand. The teachers promoted an extreme interpretation of Islam's teaching about women, ignoring Islam's explicit statements about women's value and rights. Women were described as an inferior part of humanity, to be regarded with suspicion and kept under strict control.[7]

Legions of boys thus grew up in an unnatural, all-male environment. For them the female sex was an unknown. For them religion, as taught by their ignorant teachers, provided all knowledge. They were willing to do whatever they were told: fight a "holy war" against the evil West—and beat women, another evil.

The more powerful the Taliban became, the more bizarre was the interpretation of Islam with which they tried to justify their power. Their policies toward women, they claimed, were what proved them right: total control of women was absolutely necessary and could not be modified, because it was the standard of their "legitimacy." Any backing off would be taken as a sign of weakness.[8]

We should note that the Taliban regime owed some of its success to global oil politics. In spite of the Taliban's record, an American energy company called Unocal—with support from the U.S. government—tried to do business with the Taliban.[9] By 1999, U.S. policy was reversed, thanks to pressure by American feminist and human rights groups. Nonetheless, initially the Taliban were able to confirm their harsh rule with complicity from the West.

Women Under Taliban Control

While most educated women had managed to hold up under earlier attempts to crush their independence, under the Taliban open resistance was impossible. Shut in their dark homes, in enforced idleness except for the struggle to keep their families alive, many women became dangerously depressed and suicidal. With medical care almost nonexistent,[10] infant mortality and death in childbirth became almost the highest in the world.

Women and children—primary victims of Taliban rule

Life in refugee camps was better for the hundreds of thousands of women who escaped from Afghanistan, primarily to Pakistan—but only a little better. Families with some money might rent a room in a house. That was the comparatively privileged lot of the refugee doctor and his family, now in the United States, with whom the author (EM) spoke. With four children, they had fled from western Afghanistan to Pakistan, a twenty-five-day trip on foot and donkey, over the mountains in midwinter.

The great majority of refugees lived in tents or makeshift shacks. For most refugee women, whether educated or not, there was nothing to do except prepare food for the family, if they could get it. Beset by malnutrition and health problems, in constant fear of Taliban spies and punishers, they found life almost as harsh as in Afghanistan.[11]

Afghan women and children at the Maslakh refugee camp west of Herat

Women's Reponse: Determination to Survive

A large part of Afghanistan's educated population left the country from the late 1970s on, forming an Afghan society in diaspora—scattered to many places. Among those who stayed were women who tried to preserve their culture and continue their children's schooling. In the cities, an underground education system grew up. A woman in Herat ran a secret school for 120 students, and another persuaded the Taliban to let her open a school for nurses, which soon had over 200 students. In Kabul a woman contrived to operate a network of underground schools, teaching a wide variety of subjects.[12] Secret schools also functioned in the more progressive villages; a classroom could escape notice in a traditional mud-brick house with many rooms.[13]

Running a secret school was dangerous, of course. The coming and going of students, in small groups, had to be timed so as not to attract attention. If a Taliban "enforcer" suspected that something irregular was going on in a home, he could close down the school. One woman gave up her secret school after her teenage son was severely beaten as a warning.[14]

Some schools were set up by Afghans in the refugee centers in Pakistan, but they could reach only a fraction of the children. Several women's organizations ran programs to help the women and children in camps through health clinics, education, crafts, and publications to keep women informed.

September 11 and the Aftermath for Afghanistan

The terrorist attacks on New York and Washington, D.C., on September 11, 2001, became a turning point in Afghanistan's history. Having determined that the attackers were part of the international terrorist network called Al-Qaeda, whose top leaders were sheltered by the Taliban, the United States launched a military campaign to overthrow the Taliban and wipe out the terrorist training camps in Afghanistan. The Americans worked with the forces of various Afghan leaders who had not been defeated by the Taliban, called the Northern Alliance.

In the fall of 2001, Taliban forces were routed from Kabul and other major cities, and the Northern Alliance took over. But these were some of the warlords whose fighting had nearly destroyed Afghanistan in the first place. An interim government, satisfactory to as many sides as possible, had to be set up quickly.

Sponsored by the United Nations, a council of Afghan leaders met in Bonn, Germany, in November 2001 and formed a temporary government. Three of the delegates were Afghan women, who spoke firmly about women's rights; two were chosen to head ministries in the interim government, including a ministry of women's affairs.[15] Soon after the Bonn conference, nearly fifty Afghan women gathered in Brussels, Belgium, and announced a detailed program including the demand that women's rights be included in all financial plans for reconstruction.

A *loya girga* ("grand council") met in Kabul in June 2002 to select a government to serve until 2004. More than one-tenth of the 1,600 delegates were women. Their speeches, noted as among the most eloquent and forthright, were broadcast all over the country. Some women openly confronted and chastised notorious warlords among the delegates.[16] A new era for Afghanistan's women appeared under way—at least among the elite class.

Results to Date

What about the "ordinary" women of Afghanistan? While human rights groups had been calling attention to their plight for several years, it was the American war against the Taliban that made Afghan women the world's most publicized females for a while.

Women could now appear in public without their male family escorts. They could once more seek work—although possibilities were sparse, due to the country's shattered economy. When the University of Kabul promised women half the places in the freshman class, in March 2002, throngs of girls lined up to apply.

In cities, the whole society began to breathe again, and women cautiously made their way back into the visible population. But this did not guarantee a rosy future. Many men with extremely conservative views had accepted the Taliban's way of treating women, while women in rigidly traditional areas had never experienced anything else.[17] As long as armed Northern Alliance fighters roamed the cities and countryside, men who knew nothing but fighting and taking by force, women's lives were still insecure.

And the notorious burka? In the first days after liberation from Taliban rule, U.S. newspapers showed photos of women's smiling faces, their burkas pushed back. The interim prime minister instructed ministries to hire more women and urged female government workers not to wear the burka. But real change wouldn't come easily. On International Women's Day on March 8, 2002, crowds of women in Kabul cheered the speeches—but put their burkas back on as they left the hall. Afghan women leaders emphasized that peace, safety, food, and jobs had to come first, before the matter of the burka.

Meanwhile, great numbers of people continued to live in refugee camps. They had lost their homes in the twenty-three years of fighting or had been forced out of areas stricken by drought. Adding to the Afghan people's misery was the very campaign intended to free them of Taliban rule. The bombing of Taliban strongholds by U.S. planes sometimes went tragically astray. Bombs hit villages, destroyed homes, killed many people.

Throughout the country millions of active land mines still salted the soil and caused death every day, especially among children. A generation of deeply damaged children, who knew nothing but war or camp life, were growing up with mothers emotionally crippled and fathers missing. Those young people able to return to school found they had "forgotten everything."[18]

The story of Afghanistan's long-suffering women and their efforts to forge a better future for themselves is history in the making. No one can predict what progress will be made by the hard work that must follow the declarations and promises. But this time the prospects appear to be different from the chaotic period following the Soviet withdrawal in 1989, when Western powers let a devastated Afghanistan struggle by itself. This time the world community is watching, and *must* stay involved.

> They can make us cover ourselves,
> but they cannot close our minds.
>
> —Nazir, a woman in Kabul, October 2001.[19]

16

Looking Toward Tomorrow

Where women are honored, there God is pleased.
—Arabic proverb

In this brief introduction to the lives of women in the Middle East and North Africa, we have a glimpse of great variety, along with some common features. There's no "typical" woman, of course, but one thing is clear: women are *not* the "weaker sex."

A Gathering of Voices

When Middle Eastern women think about how they look to others—specifically, the West—they usually don't like the perceived images: stereotypes, they say, based on ignorance and prejudice. But this resentment can stimulate more serious thinking about just what *are* their strengths. Let's listen in on a discussion.

In our imaginary gathering of diverse Middle Eastern women, the highly educated, self-assertive ones speak first. They express outrage at the injustices women suffer in a patriarchal society. "We *are* oppressed. I'm embarrassed by my stifling, backward culture, and I hate being pitied!"

Then others, equally educated, jump in. "We have nothing to be ashamed of. We are proud of our Middle Eastern heritage and our strong families. We don't want to be like Western women, forced to put careers and independence above love and family."

At this point, women who favor an Islam-based society will have their say. "The West is no model for us. We must return to Islam for the guide to a good society. We must find the true, Islamic way of being a woman."

Next, the idealistic, jeans-clad college students will speak. "We are modern—we don't live in tents! We can choose our boyfriends and husbands. Sure, there are problems in our society, but there are problems in every society, and ours is changing for the better. We love life—and we are not terrorists!"

Finally, quiet but steady, the village woman speaks. "We must make our own way. True happiness comes from inside, and we will find it only when we realize our own strengths."

Femininity

Middle Eastern women are strong. Yet within their strength lies femininity, too. Women pride themselves on their cooking and homemaking, their ability to please their husbands, and their appearance. While this may seem unliberated to many Americans, Middle Eastern society still encourages women to express themselves in this way, regardless of what else they may do or achieve.

On the streets of Beirut, Tunis, and Istanbul, for example, pride in dress is evident. Even modest Islamic dress can make a striking fashion statement. And dress can say much more. At a Middle Eastern airport, boarding a flight to

New York, the author (EM) once met a woman whose face appeared aged by a life of hard work but who wore a full-length gown exquisitely embroidered in the traditional Palestinian style. When I complimented her in Arabic, she indicated that she had made it herself. This uneducated village woman, traveling alone to a strange land, presented herself with courage and obvious pride in her culture.

The Struggle for Change

Middle Eastern women's struggle for a better life takes different forms. Some, like the women of the Islamist movement, find strength in their religious identity and firmly held religious views. Others aim at reforming the patriarchal values of Middle Eastern society. That's a long, tough road—but along with the obstacles, there are occasionally surprising successes. Take, for instance, a setback in Kuwait in 2001, when Islamists demanded that a women's soccer match be canceled because God would be offended by men watching those young female bodies.[1] Yet in Saudi Arabia in 2000, a Saudi woman surgeon successfully performed a first-ever type of organ transplant, heading a team of male doctors.[2]

Whether they call themselves "feminist" or not, women in many Middle Eastern societies seek change in personal-status laws, greater political power for women, and enlightenment in popular attitudes. Activists for women's causes are still a tiny minority, but they are not solitary voices in the wilderness. The walls of "hush-hush," which prevent people from dealing with problems of a personal nature, are starting to crack. Where given the chance to air their concerns about a wide range of sensitive subjects, both women and men are starting to open up. Television and radio call-in shows get an eager response.

An Egyptian election campaign poster proclaims "I love the life of freedom."

Although most governments are already investing considerably in areas that affect women's lives, far more needs to be done regarding reform of legal systems, encouragement of employment opportunities, and effective family planning programs. But in some countries—Egypt, Algeria, Saudi Arabia, Iran—governments are under pressure from the opposite direction, the Islamists who raise strident voices against rights for women. The outlook is complex and uncertain.

Another challenge is finding the best way to work together. If women advance primarily as individuals—with a higher academic degree, a better job—then empowerment of the female population as a whole will make slow progress. Both differences and indifference must be overcome—and also the desire of many individuals always to have the loudest voice in the room.

Tradition and Change

Rapidly changing societies make heavy and often contradictory demands on women. Yet many Middle Eastern women are meeting the challenge and making their voices heard. Is this the direction of the future, or will backward pressures manage to return women to their "proper place" as second-class citizens? If women succeed in throwing off the constraints of tradition, will they also lose the sustaining bonds of family, culture, and community? For years to come, the forces of tradition and change will continue in battle, across the field of women's lives in the Middle East and North Africa.

Notes

Chapter Two

1. Dalenda Largueche, conversation with author, Tunis, February 1995.

2. Douglas Jehl, "It's Barbie vs. Laila and Sara in Mideast Culture War," *New York Times*, June 2, 1999.

3. Susan Schaeffer Davis, "Growing Up in Morocco," in Donna Bowen and Evelyn Early, eds., *Everyday Life in the Muslim Middle East*, 2nd. ed. (Bloomington: Indiana University Press, 2001), 33.

Chapter Three

1. Asma Yahya al-Basha, "Women in Yemen—Past and Present," in Werner Daum, *Yemen: 3000 Years of Art and Civilization in Arabia Felix* (Frankfurt/Main, Germany: Penguin, 1988), 392.

2. Edith Hanania, *Arab Women and Education* (Beirut: Institute for Women's Studies in the Arab World, 1980), 17.

3. Marnia Lazreq, *The Eloquence of Silence: Algerian Women in Question* (London: Routledge, 1994), 63–79.

4. Sheikha al-Misnad, *The Development of Modern Education in the Gulf* (London: Ithaca Press, 1985), 37–38, 41.

5. *UNESCO Statistical Yearbook* (Paris, 1993), Tables 3.1, 3.4, 3.7.

6. Orayb Aref Najjar and Kitty Warnock, *Portraits of Palestinian Women* (Salt Lake City: University of Utah Press, 1992), 14–15. Also, Walid Khalidi, *Before Their Diaspora: A Photographic History of the Palestinians 1876–1948* (Washington, D.C.: Institute for Palestine Studies, 1984), 71.

7. "Libya Invests in Its People's Education," *Washington Report on Middle East Affairs*, vol. 20, no. 2 (March 2001), 58. Also, Julinda

Abu Nasr, et al., *Identification and Elimination of Sex Stereotypes in School Textbooks* (Beirut: Institute of Women's Studies in the Arab World, 1983).

8. Children's books publisher, Librairie du Liban, conversation with author, Beirut, March 1995.

9. Youth worker and teachers, conversations with author, Beirut, February 2002.

10. May Seikaly, "Women and Social Change in Bahrain," *International Journal of Middle East Studies*, vol. 26, no. 3 (August 1994), 420.

11. Nasriee Hekmat-Farrokh, conversation with author, Bloomington, IN, June 1995.

12. Nabil Alnawwab, United Nations Specialist in Social Development Issues and Policies, interview with author, Beirut, February 2002.

13. PBS program on Tunisia, aired September 8, 1994.

14. Microsoft Encarta Encyclopedia, 2001.

15. "A Lifetime Commitment: Aicha Barki," *UNESCO Sources*, Issue 94 (October 1997), 5.

16. "Only Very Few Girls Even Start to Go to School in Yemen," from *Choices*, United Nations Development Program, reported in Women's International Network News, vol. 23, no. 3 (Summer 1997), 52.

17. Peace Corps volunteer (Morocco, 1999–2000), letter to author, January 2002.

CHAPTER FOUR

1. See "The Koran on the Subject of Women," in Elizabeth W. Fernea and Basima Bezirgan, eds., *Middle Eastern Women Speak* (Austin: University of Texas Press, 1977), 7–26.

2. The Qur'an, suras 2:228 and 4:34.

3. Fatima Mernissi, *Beyond the Veil: Male-Female Dynamics in Modern Muslim Society* (Bloomington: Indiana University Press, 1987), Introduction and Ch. 1.

4. Cheryl A. Rubenberg, *Palestinian Women: Patriarchy and Resistance in the West Bank* (Boulder, CO: Lynne Rienner), 232–38.

5. See Dale F. Eickelman, "Inside the Islamic Reformation," in Bowen and Early, op. cit., Ch. 22.

6. Nayereh Tohidi, "Islamic Feminism: Perils and Promises," paper presented at a conference on "Middle Eastern Women on the Move," Woodrow Wilson International Center for Scholars, Washington, D.C., October 2–3, 2001.

CHAPTER FIVE

1. Muna Hamzeh, conversation with author, Austin, TX, November 2001.

2. Chris Hedges, "Fleeing the Mullah's Men for Hijinks in the Hills," *New York Times International,* August 8, 1994.

3. Brooke Anderson, letter to author from Damascus, January 2002. Author's observations in Beirut and Cairo.

4. Maha Nureddine, conversation with authors, Bloomington, IN, September 1994.

5. Alnawwab, interview.

6. Peace Corps volunteer (Morocco), letter. See also Lazreq, op. cit., 173.

7. Julia Droeber, communication to author from Exeter, UK, January 2002.

8. Rana Husseini, "Crimes of Honor," *Al-Raida,* vol. XVII, no. 89 (Spring 2000), 19.

9. "Rana Husseini Discusses Crimes of Honor in Jordan," *Washington Report on Middle East Affairs,* vol. 19, no. 4 (May 2000), 99.

10. Rana Husseini, personal communication from Amman, July 2002.

11. Michael Gorkin and Rafiqa Othman, *Three Mothers, Three Daughters* (Berkeley: University of California Press, 1996), 49.

Chapter Six

1. Bouthaina Shaaban, *Both Right and Left Handed: Arab Women Talk About Their Lives* (Bloomington: Indiana University Press, 1988), 15.

2. "Islamic Family Law Tabulated" (chart), *Al-Raida*, vol. XVIII–XIX, nos. 93–94 (Spring–Summer 2001): 65–69. Also, William J. Goode, *World Change in Divorce Patterns* (New Haven: Yale University Press, 1993), 264.

3. Ali Ghalem, *A Wife for my Son* (New York: Banner Press, 1984), 74.

4. Judy H. Brink, "Changing Extended Family Relationships in an Egyptian Village," *Urban Anthropology*, vol. 16, no. 2 (1987), 138.

5. Christine Eickelman, "Oil, Fertility, and Women's Status in Oman," in Bowen and Early, op. cit., 131.

6. Ayse Gürsan-Salzmann, "The Women of Yassahoyuk, Turkey: Changing Roles in a New Economy," *Expedition*, vol. 43, no. 3 (2001), 23.

7. Mohammad Awadh Baobaid, "Police Response to Violence Against Women: Yemen as a Case Study," *Al-Raida*, vol. XVII, no. 89 (Spring 2000), 38–40.

8. Personal information obtained at the Center for Help for Women Victims of Violence in Tunis, from Peace Corps volunteers in Morocco, and from Lebanese and Algerian activists in Beirut. See also Rubenberg, op. cit., 213.

9. Nazik Yared, conversations with author, Beirut, 1995, 2002. See also Myriam Sfeir, "A Council Resisting Violence Against Women," *Al-Raida*, vol. XVII, no. 89 (Spring 2000), 35–36.

10. Amal Altoma, conversation with author, Bloomington, IN, May 1995.

11. Goode, op. cit., 271.

12. "Divorce Iranian Style," documentary film by Kim Longinotto and Ziba Mir-Hoseini, 1997.

13. Shaaban, op. cit., 68.

14. Goode, op. cit., 272. Also, personal information from a Lebanese-Canadian researcher, Beirut, 1995.

Chapter Seven

1. Regarding Algerian Family Law, see Lazreq, op. cit., 150–57.
2. "Women and the Law in Lebanon," *Al-Raida*, vol. IX, no. 49 (May 1990), 3–6. Also, Lamia Shehadeh, conversation with author, Beirut, March 1995.
3. *Women and Men in the Arab Region: A Statistical Portrait, 2000* (UNESCO, 1999), 20.
4. Ibid., 25. Also, information supplied by the Population Council in Cairo, 1995.
5. Consultant to Peace Corp, conversation with author, Tunis, January 1995.
6. George Moffett, "The Good News About Population Growth," *Choice: The Human Development Magazine*, United Nations Development Program (September 1994), 19.
7. Christine Eickelman, op. cit., 130.
8. Lecture by Dr. Lila Abu-Lughod, Cairo, December 1989.
9. "Survey of women's conditions and rights in Syria," document from the Syrian Embassy, Washington, D.C. (no author or date).
10. Marta Paluch, *Yemeni Voices: Women Tell Their Stories* (Sana'a, Yemen: British Council, 2001), 19–20.
11. Nihad Hamadi, conversation with authors, Bloomington, IN, August 1994.

Chapter Eight

1. Fadwa el Guindi, *Veil: Modesty, Privacy and Resistance* (Oxford: Berg, 1999), 172. See also, Haleh Esfandiari, *Reconstructed Lives: Women and Iran's Islamic Revolution* (Washington, D.C.: Woodrow Wilson Center Press, 1997), 146, 149.
2. The Qur'an, sura 24:31.
3. "Legendary Trails: The Gift of Incense," PBS television program, December 16, 1994.

4. See Arlene Elowe MacLeod, "Hegemonic Relations and Gender Resistance: The New Veiling as Accommodating Protest in Cairo," *Signs*, vol. 17, no. 3 (1992).

5. el Guindi, op. cit., 145.

6. Elizabeth Fernea, "The Veiled Revolution," in Bowen and Early, op. cit., 152.

7. Najat Ismail, conversation with author, Cairo, October 1995.

8. Judith Harik, conversation with author, Beirut, March 1995.

9. Alnawwab, interview.

10. Stated clearly in Sheikh al-Sha'rawi's published views on women: see Barbara Freyer Stowasser, "Religious Ideology, Women, and the Family: The Islamic Paradigm," in Barbara Freyer Stowasser, ed., *The Islamic Impulse* (Washington, D.C.: Center for Contemporary Arab Studies, 1987), 270–77. Another reference is Fouad Zakaria, "The Standpoint of Contemporary Muslim Fundamentalists," in Nahid Toubia, ed., *Women of the Arab World: The Coming Challenge* (London: Zed Books, 1988), 31–35.

CHAPTER NINE

1. "Health Promotion Behaviors of Jordanian Women," *Health Care for Women International*, vol. 20, no. 6 (November/December 1999), 533ff.

2. Paluch, op. cit., 121–23.

3. "Women in Development," 2001 World Development Indicators, World Bank.

4. Laurie King-Irani, "Women and AIDS in Lebanon," *Al-Raida*, vol. XIII, nos. 74 and 75 (Summer/Fall 1996), 49–51.

5. Heba Hage, "Female Circumcision: Culture or Torture?" *Al-Raida*, vol. XIII, no. 72 (Winter 1996), 40–41.

6. *An-Nahar* (Cairo), February 6 and May 22, 1997; reported in *Al-Raida*, vol. XIV, no. 77 (Spring 1997), 8.

7. Nayra Atiya, *Khul-Khaal: Five Egyptian Women Tell Their Stories* (Syracuse: Syracuse University Press, 1982), 11.

8. Nahid Toubia, "Women and Health in Sudan," in *Toubia*, op. cit., 102.

9. Alifa Rifaat, *Distant View of a Minaret* (London: Quartet Books, 1983), 100.

10. Fran Hosken, "Stop Female Genital Mutilation: Women Speak," Women's International Network News, 1995. Also, "The Egyptian FGM Task Force: A Singular Vision with a Plurality of Dimensions," *Awaken*, online publication of Equality Now, 1998 (www.equalitynow.org/review_brochure_eng_ awaken.html). In addition, Marie Assad, conversation with author, Cairo, November 1995.

CHAPTER TEN

1. Souad Chater, *Les Emancipées du Harem: Regard sur la Femme Tunisienne* (Tunis: 1992), 124–32.

2. "La Femme Tunisienne en Chiffres," Center of Research, Documentation, and Information on Women (Ministry of Women and Family, Tunis, 1994), 9.

3. Valentine M. Moghadam, *Women, Work, and Economic Reform in the Middle East and North Africa* (Boulder, CO: Lynne Rienner, 1998), 93.

4. "All It Takes Is a Dream," *Middle East*, Issue 308 (January 2001), 48.

5. Samira Harboush, "Nontraditional Training for Women in the Arab World," *Africa Report*, vol. 26, no. 2 (March 1981).

6. Barbara Lethem Ibrahim, "Cairo's Factory Women," in Elizabeth W. Fernea, ed., *Women and the Family in the Middle East* (Austin: University of Texas Press, 1985), 293–99.

7. Chater, op. cit., 102.

8. Moghadam, *Women, Work* . . . , op. cit., 73.

9. Jane Kokan, "In Love with Qaddafi," *BBC Focus on Africa*, vol. VI, no. 3 (July–September 1995), 4–8.

10. Fatiha Akeb and Malika Abdelaziz, "Algerian Women Discuss the Need for Change," in Fernea, ed., *Women and the Family...*, op. cit., 9, 270.

11. Nada Awar, "An Artist's Search for an Intense Serenity: A Conversation with Painter Helen Khal," *Al-Raida*, vol. XIII, no. 73 (Spring 1996), 16.

12. Conversations with young Lebanese and Jordanian women, 2002.

13. Louisa Ait Hamou, conversation with author, Tunis, January 1995.

14. Discussion at a workshop for women in managerial positions, sponsored by Fulbright Commission, Cairo, November 1995.

15. Valentine M. Maghadam, *Modernizing Women: Gender and Social Change in the Middle East* (Boulder, CO: Lynne Rienner, 1993), 205–06.

16. Nadia Hijab, "Women and Work in the Arab World," Middle East Research and Information Project (MERIP), 1994, 6.

17. Moghadam, "Women, Work, and Ideology in the Islamic Republic," *International Journal of Middle East Studies*, vol. 20, no. 2 (May 1988), 238.

18. See, for example, "Saudi Arabian Women Dispel Myths and Stereotypes," *Washington Report on Middle East Affairs*, vol. 20, no. 4 (May/June 2001), 35.

19. See *Al-Raida*, vol. X, no. 64 (Winter 1994).

CHAPTER ELEVEN

1. Bouthaina Shaaban, "The Hidden World of Arab Feminism," *Ms.* (May/June 1993), 76–77.

2. Laurence Deonna, *On Persian Roads* (Pueblo, CO: Passeggiata Press, 1999), 54.

3. Farzaneh Milani, introd., *Stories by Iranian Women Since the Revolution* (Austin: University of Texas Press, 1991).

4. See, for example, Evelyn Accad, *Veil of Shame: The Role of Women in the Contemporary Fiction of North Africa and the Arab World* (Sherbrooke, Quebec: Naaman, 1978); Margot Badran and Miriam Cooke, *Opening the Gates: A Century of Arab Feminist Writing* (Bloomington: Indiana University Press, 1990); Saddeka Arebi, *Women and Words in Saudi Arabia: The Politics of a Literary*

Discourse (New York: Columbia University Press, 1994).

5. Miriam Cooke, *War's Other Voices: Women Writers on the Lebanese Civil War* (Cambridge: Cambridge University Press, 1987).

6. "A Spaceship of Tenderness to the Moon" by Layla Ba'labakki, "An Account of Her Trial on Charges of Obscenity and Endangering Public Morality," in Fernea and Bezirgan, op. cit. The other novel is Hanan al-Shaykh, *The Story of Zahra* (London: Readers International, 1992).

7. "Talking 'bout My Generation," *Middle East*, no. 306 (November 2000), 47.

8. There have been some exceptions to this rule, notably Persian and Turkish miniature painting.

9. Salwa Mikdadi Nashashibi, *Forces of Change: Artists of the Arab World*, Arab Women Artists Exhibit (Washington, D.C.: National Museum of Women in the Arts, 1994), 19–20, 25, 30.

10. See Nada Awar, "Female Singers in the Arab World: Cultural Symbols in a Traditional Society," *Al-Raida*, vol. IX, no. 51 (November 1990).

11. Camelia Entekhabi-Fard, "Behind the Veil," *Mother Jones*, vol. 26, no. 4 (July/August 2001), 68.

12. Wendy Buonaventura, *Serpent of the Nile: Women and Dance in the Arab World* (New York: Interlink Books, 1990), 196, 200–202.

13. *Al-Raida*, vol. XVI, nos. 86-87 (Summer/Fall 1999) is devoted to "Arab Women and Cinema."

14. Geraldine Brooks, *Nine Parts of Desire: The Hidden World of Islamic Women* (New York: Anchor Books/Doubleday, 1995), 201–ll.

15. Roslyn Dupre, "Sahar El Hawarri, Egypt," *Women's Sports and Fitness*, vol. 19, no. 8 (October 1997), 63.

CHAPTER TWELVE

1. Haya al-Mughini, *Women in Kuwait: The Politics of Gender* (London: Saqi Books, 1993), 145–48. "All Roads Lead to the Franchise," *UNESCO Courier* (March 2001), 4–9.

2. Heba el-Shazli, "The Performance of Women in the Egyptian Parliamentary Elections of 2000," *Al-Raida*, vol. XVIII, no. 92 (Winter 2001), 49.

3. "Nayla Moawad: On Politics in Lebanon," *Al-Raida*, vol. XVIII, no. 92 (Winter 2001), 47–48.

4. Marguerite Helou, "Lebanese Women and Politics," *Al-Raida*, vol. XVIII, no. 92 (Winter 2001), 35, 37, 39–40.

5. Haleh Esfandiari, *Reconstructed Lives: Women and Iran's Islamic Revolution* (Baltimore: Johns Hopkins University Press, 1997), 46, 210–11.

6. Lazreq, op. cit. Ch. 7.

7. BBC news broadcast, Middle East Service, May 5, 1995.

8. Cover photo, *Realites* magazine (Tunis), no. 481, January 13–19, 1995.

9. Lamia Rustum Shehadeh, ed., *Women and War in Lebanon* (Gainesville: University Press of Florida, 1999), Ch. 9.

10. Bouthaina Shaaban, op. cit., 92–101. Also, Shehadeh, op. cit., Ch. 10.

11. Laure Abi-Saleh and Laudy Harik, conversations with author, Beirut, March 1995.

12. Ghena Ismail, "The Unsung Heroines of Lebanon," *Al-Raida*, vol. XIII, no. 72 (Winter 1996): 22–23.

13. Rana Salibi, "Women's Activities in Popular Committees During the Intifada," in Ebba Augustin, ed., *Palestinian Women: Identity and Experience* (London: Zed Books, 1993), 167.

14. Philippa Strum, "The Palestinian Women's Movement," paper presented at the conference "Middle Eastern Women on the Move," Woodrow Wilson Center, October 2–3, 2001, 5.

15. Libby Brooks, "We Just Want to Live Normally," *The Guardian* (January 29, 2002).

Chapter Thirteen

1. Document supplied by the Syrian Embassy, op. cit. Also, Sarah Graham-Brown, "New Writings on Women, Politics, and Social

Change," *Middle East Report 173*, vol. 21, no. 6 (November/December 1991), 33. Regarding Iraq, see Elizabeth Fernea, *In Search of Islamic Feminism* (New York: Doubleday, 1998), 295–96, 320.

2. Nadia Hijab, "Jordanian Women: A Programme with a Difference," United Nations Population Fund (New York: United Nations, 1989), 19.

3. Personal communication from a Peace Corps volunteer in Morocco, 2002, and Algerian scholars, 1995 and 2002. Also, "A Chance for a New Life," *UNESCO Sources*, no. 131 (February 2001), 22.

4. Nadia Farah, "The Egyptian Women's Health Book Collective," *Middle East Report 173*, vol. 21, no. 6 (November/December 1991).

5. Interview with Eileen Kuttab, director of the Women Studies Institute at Birzeit University, *Al-Raida*, vol. XVII–XVIII, nos. 90–91 (Summer/Fall 2000), 21.

6. *Centerpoint*, newsletter of the Woodrow Wilson International Center for Scholars, Washington, D.C. (December 2001), 1.

7. Paluch, op. cit., 119.

8. For a survey of the Egyptian women's movement, see *Al-Raida*, vol. XVIII, no. 92 (Winter 2001), 12.

9. Strum, op. cit., 4, 15.

10. Rubenberg, op. cit., 240, 242–43.

11. Haideh Moghissi, *Populism and Feminism in Iran* (New York: St. Martin's Press, 1994), 183–85. Also, Esfandiari, op. cit., 144.

12. Amy Waldman, "In Iran, an Angry Generation Longs for Jobs, More Freedom and Power," *New York Times*, December 7, 2001, p. A10. Also, December 8, 2001, p. A8.

13. Elizabeth W. Fernea, *In Search of Islamic Feminism*, op. cit., 80–81. See also, Rania al-Abiad, "A Turbulent Morocco," *Al-Raida*, vol. XVII, no. 89 (Spring 2000), 30–34.

14. Tohidi, op. cit., 4. See also, Janet Afary, "Portraits of Two Islamist Women: Escape from Freedom or from Tradition?" *Critique*, no. 19 (Fall 2001).

Chapter Fourteen

1. Fatima Mernissi, *Beyond the Veil: Male-Female Dynamics in Modern Muslim Society* (Bloomington: Indiana University Press, 1987), 129–31.
2. Gorkin and Othman, op. cit., 27.
3. "Gender Relations and Development in the Yemen," *Peacekeeping and International Relations*, vol. 28, no. 3 (May/June 1999), section on "Women's Productive Activities in the Rural Sector: Animal Husbandry."
4. "Caring Institutions in Lebanon," *Al-Raida*, vol. XVI, no. 85 (Spring 1999), 35–38.
5. Magda Iskander, "Care With Love Training Program," *Al-Raida*, vol. XVI, no. 85 (Spring 1999), 57–58.
6. *Women and Men . . . A Statistical Portrait . . .* , op. cit., 11, 12, 14.
7. Lila Abu-Lughod, "Islam and the Gendered Discourse of Death," *International Journal of Middle Eastern Studies*, vol. 25 (May 1993), 187–205.

Chapter Fifteen

1. Ahmed Rashid, *Taliban: Militant Islam, Oil and Fundamentalism in Central Asia* (New Haven, CT: Yale University Press, 2000), 217.
2. Fahima Rahimi, *Women in Afghanistan* (Liestal: Bibliotheca Afghanica, 1986), 42, 44, 46.
3. Deborah Ellis, *Women of the Afghan War* (Westport, CT: Praeger, 2000), 42–43.
4. Jan Goodwin, "Buried Alive: Afghan Women Under the Taliban," *On the Issues* (online), vol. 7, no. 3 (Summer 1998), 10.
5. Rashid, op. cit., 82.
6. Ibid., 101, 222–25.
7. Ibid., 32–33.
8. Ibid., 111.
9. Ibid., 163, 165–69, 177–82.
10. See Bob Herbert, "A Doctor's Story," *New York Times*, December 27, 2001, p. A19.
11. Ellis, op. cit., chapter on "Camp Life," 73–95.

12. Amy Waldman, "Behind the Burka: Women Subtly Fought Taliban," *New York Times,* November 19, 2001, p. A1. Also, Richard Lacayo, "About Face: An Inside Look at How Women Fared Under Taliban Oppression . . . ," *Time,* vol. 158, no. 24 (December 3, 2001), 46.

13. Gene Stoltzfuss (Christian Peacemakers Team member who visited Afghanistan in January 2002), telephone conversation with author, February 2002.

14. Jon Lee Anderson, "City of Dreams," *The New Yorker* (December 24 and 31, 2001), 51.

15. *New York Times,* December 5, 2001, p. B4, and December 8, 2001, p. B3.

16. Pamela Constable, "Delegates Give Karzai a Diversity of Advice," Washington Post Foreign Service, June 15, 2002, p. A18.

17. Norimitsu Onishi, "In New Leader's Village, Taliban Rules Are Just Tradition," *New York Times,* December 22, 2001, p. B1.

18. Barry Bearak, "Escaping Afghanistan, Children Pay Price," *New York Times,* October 30, 2001, p. B1.

19. Lois Raimondo, "Armed with needles and thread, Afghan women work for rights, food," *The Washington Post,* reprinted in *Savannah Morning News,* October 21, 2001.

CHAPTER SIXTEEN

1. "Women's Sports Raise Ire in Kuwait," *Christian Science Monitor,* vol. 93, no. 93 (April 9, 2001), 9.

2. *New York Times,* March 7, 2001, p. A1.

Glossary

abbayah—A woman's black cloak that covers the wearer from head to foot, as worn by women in the Arabian Peninsula and Gulf states; called *chador* in Iraq and Iran.

Allah—The Arabic word for God, meaning the God of biblical tradition.

Bedouin—Nomads, people who move about with their flocks, usually with no permanent place of residence.

conservative—Tending to resist change and preserve existing conditions, ideas, and customs. The opposite tendency—openness to change and to new ideas and interpretations—can be described as liberal or progressive.

fundamentalism—Belief in strict, often literal, interpretation of the creed and rules of a religion.

harem—In traditional Muslim societies, the part of a household where the women lived and carried on their activities.

hijab—Literally, "cover": the practice of covering a woman's hair and body, and in some societies her face, for the sake of modesty and adherence to religious and social requirements; often referred to as "veiling" or "the veil."

Islam—The monotheistic religion started by Muhammad early in the seventh century A.D., in Arabia. The basic beliefs call for "submission" (the literal meaning of *Islam*) to the will of God. Islam recognizes the revelations of

Judaism and Christianity as forerunners of the ultimate religious truth revealed by Muhammad.

Islamism—Belief in Islam and Islamic values as the source of proper behavior for individuals, society, and government.

Levant—The countries of the eastern Mediterranean: Syria, Lebanon, Palestine; the word comes from the French word for "rise" and suggests the rising of the sun in the east.

mahr—Money and goods that a man gives to his bride, the amount of which is usually stipulated by her family; sometimes called "bride wealth."

mosque—A house of worship for the Islamic religion; in form, a mosque can range from a single room to a magnificent building.

Muhammad—The Prophet of Islam. Muhammad, who lived from approximately A.D 570 to 632, was originally a merchant in the Arabian city of Mecca; in his fortieth year, according to Muslim belief, he started to receive God's messages for humankind and preached this message to his ever-increasing followers. The name can also be spelled in other ways, such as Mohammed.

Muslim—A follower of the Islamic religion: "One who submits (to the will of God)."

patriarchy—A form of social organization in which men are supreme, with women kept dependent on them and generally in an inferior position.

pilgrimage—A visit, usually involving a journey, to a place considered sacred.

polygamy—Multiple simultaneous marriages; the specific term for having multiple *wives* is polygyny.

Qur'an—The holy book of Islam; Muslims believe that it was entirely revealed to Muhammad by an angel from God. Literally the word, also spelled Koran, means "the reading."

shari'a—The Islamic code of laws, based on the Qur'an, Muhammad's teachings and example, and interpretations by later Muslim judges and scholars.

stereotype—A conventional, oversimplified idea or image that disregards individual characteristics and variations.

tradition—Custom, practice, belief handed down from one generation of a group to the next, orally or by example, and often with a binding effect.

Selected Bibliography

Abu-Lughod, Lila. *Writing Women's World: Bedouin Stories.* Berkeley: University of California Press, 1992.

Ahmed, Laila. *Women and Gender in Islam.* New Haven: Yale University Press, 1992.

Atiya, Nayra. *Khul-Khaal: Five Egyptian Women Tell Their Stories.* Syracuse: Syracuse University Press, 1982.

Augustin, Ebba. *Palestinian Women: Identity and Experience.* London: Zed Books, 1993.

Bowen, Donna Lee, and Early, Evelyn A., eds. *Everyday Life in the Muslim Middle East,* second edition. Bloomington: Indiana University Press, 2002.

Deonna, Laurence. *On Persian Roads: Glimpses of Revolutionary Iran, 1985–1998.* Pueblo, CO: Passeggiata Press, 1999.

Early, Evelyn A. *Baladi Women of Cairo.* Boulder, CO: Lynn Rienner, 1993.

Ellis, Deborah. *Women of the Afghan War.* Westport, CT: Praeger, 2000.

_____. *The Breadwinner* (novel). Toronto: Groundwood Books/Douglas & McIntyre, 2000.

_____. *Parvana's Journey* (novel). Toronto: Douglas and McIntyre, 2002.

Esfandiari, Haleh. *Reconstructed Lives: Women and Iran's Islamic Revolution.* Washington, D.C.: Woodrow Wilson Center Press, 1997.

Fernea, Elizabeth Warnock. *In Search of Islamic Feminism: One Woman's Global Journey.* New York: Doubleday, 1998.

————, ed. *Women and Family in the Middle East.* Austin: University of Texas Press, 1985.

el Guindi, Fadwa. *Veil: Modesty, Privacy and Resistance.* Oxford: Berg, 1999.

Hamzeh, Muna. *Refugees in Our Own Land: Chronicles from a Palestinian Refugee Camp in Bethlehem.* London: Pluto Press, 2001.

Gorkin, Michael, and Othman, Rafiqa. *Three Mothers, Three Daughters: Palestinian Women's Stories.* Berkeley: University of California Press, 1996.

Lateef, Nelda. *Women of Lebanon: Interviews with Champions for Peace.* Jefferson, NC: McFarland, 1997.

Lazreq, Marnia. *The Eloquence of Silence: Algerian Women in Question.* London: Routledge, 1994.

Mernissi, Fatima. *The Harem Within.* London: Doubleday, 1994.

Milaneh, Fatima. *Veils and Words: The Emerging Voices of Iranian Women Writers.* Syracuse: Syracuse University Press, 1993.

Moghadam, Valentine M. *Women, Work, and Economic Reform in the Middle East and North Africa.* Boulder: Lynne Rienner, 1998.

Nashat, Guity, and Tucker, Judith E. *Women in the Middle East and North Africa.* Bloomington: Indiana University Press, 1999.

Rashid, Ahmed. *Taliban: Militant Islam, Oil, and Fundamentalism in Central Asia.* New Haven: Yale University Press, 2000.

Shaaban, Bouthaina. *Both Right and Left Handed: Arab Women Talk About Their Lives.* Bloomington: Indiana University Press, 1991.

Sullivan, Earl L. *Women in Egyptian Public Life.* Syracuse: Syracuse University Press, 1986.

Watson, Helen. *Women in the City of the Dead.* Trenton: Africa World Press, 1992.

Journals

Al-Raida. Institute for Women's Studies in the Arab World, Lebanese American University, Beirut, Lebanon.

International Journal of Middle East Studies. Middle East Studies Association of North America: Cambridge University Press.

Saudi Aramco World. Aramco Services Company, Houston.

Web Sites

A sample of Web sites pertaining to women's organizations and activities.

Association for Middle East Women's Studies
www.amews.org
Besides information about this scholarly/professional organization, the site includes links to numerous women's organizations in the Middle East/North Africa.

Aviva
www.aviva.org
An online magazine of news, events, and resources about women everywhere, including the Middle East.

Revolutionary Association of the Women of Afghanistan
www.rawa.org
An independent political/social women's organization working for human rights and support of Afghan women victims of war and repression.

Women's Studies Center
www.wameed.org
A Palestinian Web site concerned with research on women's issues; includes a list of many women's organizations in other countries.

Index

abbayah (clothing), 29, 86
actors, 120–121
Adnan, Etel, 116
Afghan Women's Association, *138*
Afghanistan, 17
  Al-Qaeda terrorist network, 159
  burkas (clothing), 153, 160–161
  childbirth deaths, 156
  confinement in, 156
  Department of the Promotion of
    Virtue and Prevention of Vice,
    153–154, *154*
  education in, 151, 152, 155, 158
  employment in, 151, 153
  history of, 150
  home life in, *79*
  hospitals in, *94*
  infant mortality rate, 156
  International Women's Day, 160–161
  ministry of women's affairs, 159
  mujahhideen, 152
  Northern Alliance, 159, 160
  Pashtun tribe, 154–155
  refugee camps, 157, *157*, 158, 161
  September 11 attack and, 159–160
  Soviet invasion of, 151–152
  Taliban, 150, 152, 154–157
  voting rights, 151
'A'isha, wife of Muhammad, 116
Al-Qaeda terrorist network, 159
Al-Raida magazine, 137
Algeria
  abuse support centers in, 63
  education in, 25–26
  "Iqraa!" program, 34
  political activism in, 128–129
  voting rights in, 125
  women's unions in, 136
  writers in, 115
Algerian White (Assia Djebar), 128
Almaast, Hala, *117*
American University of Cairo, 138
American University of Beirut, 31, *32*,
  105, 122
Amyuni, Rima, 118
"Arab Women and Literary Creativity"
  conference, 116

Arab Women's Book Fair, 115
Arab Women's Solidarity Association,
  136
Arab Women's Summit, *127*
architecture, 117
art, *113*, *117*
  architecture, 117
  crafts, 117
  needlecraft, 118
  "stitchery pictures," *113*, 118
  weaving, *113*, 118
Ashrawi, Hanan, 132, 140

Bahithat (female researchers), 116
"Bahiyya's Eyes" (Alifa Rifaat), 98
Bahrain
  education in, 31
  women's unions in, 136
Barbie dolls, 20
bathhouses, 77, 153
Bedouins
  children, 22
  marriage, 60
  veiling, 85
Beijing Conference for Women's
  Development, 139
"belly dancing," 120
Birzeit University, 137
burkas (clothing), 153, 160–161

Cairo Family Planning Association, 98
Cairo University, 31
"Care With Love" program, 148
Center for Research, In Study,
  Documentation, and Information on
  Women (CREDIF), 137
Center of Arab Women for Training
  and Research (CAWTAR), 137
chador (clothing), 87
charitable organizations, 134–135
cheek-kissing custom, 20
children, *19*, *21*, *23*, *61*, *157*
  affection with relatives, 20
  born out of wedlock, 53
  custody laws, 65–66
  day-care centers, 107, 108
  employment of, 21